Youn

POETRY C(

GREAT MINDS

- 9

ur World...Your Future...YOUR WORDS

- Verse-Atility

Edited by Michelle Afford

821

YoungWriters

First published in Great Britain in 2005 by:
Young Writers
Remus House
Coltsfoot Drive
Peterborough
PE2 9JX
Telephone: 01733 890066
Website: www.youngwriters.co.uk

SB ISBN 1 84602 314 9

Foreword

This year, the Young Writers' 'Great Minds' competition proudly presents a showcase of the best poetic talent selected from over 40,000 up-and-coming writers nationwide.

Young Writers was established in 1991 to promote the reading and writing of poetry within schools and to the youth of today. Our books nurture and inspire confidence in the ability of young writers and provide a snapshot of poems written in schools and at home by budding poets of the future.

The thought, effort, imagination and hard work put into each poem impressed us all and the task of selecting poems was a difficult but nevertheless enjoyable experience.

We hope you are as pleased as we are with the final selection and that you and your family continue to be entertained with *Great Minds - Verse-Atility* for many years to come.

Contents

Downfield Sixth Form

English Martyrs Catholic School, Leicester

The Poems

The Garden Of Dreams

The garden of dreams is found in a park by a riverbed,
All the flowers in the garden are alive, and never dead.
The garden softly glistens because of the big wide lake,
The more it glistens the flowers grow quicker and look extremely fake.

For every person that goes in comes out with a smile on their face,
Due to a magical feeling that excites the best of space.
Every leaf that belongs to a tree holds a dream we dream,
For every leaf that floats along carries the dream like a stream.
Bad dreams, good dreams, all the dreams there are,
Big ones, small ones, long ones, short ones, dreams from afar.
People come to the garden because it is so safe and clean,
All the flowers and dreams are the best of the best ever seen.
The sun rays always gleam and never go to sleep,
Because the love of the dreams go so deep for the tiny particles do peep.

The dreams last forever for the garden keeps them well,
And that is good, for the wind blows the garden like a swinging golden bell.

The life of the garden is so important for the dreams to live and be,
And it is important because the happy dreams were once a part of you and me.
So go to the park by the riverbed and see a glistening stream,
And you'll know straight away that it's 'the garden of dreams'.

Kayleigh Veentjer (14)

Monsoon

Is the monsoon nearly over?
He has danced on my shoulders,
For six months and a week,
Sprinkling the village with the delicacy
Of violin fingers.
And still,
The deluge continues,
Oozing with passion,
Dampening the love,
And turning the mills of fervour.
In the West,
He has watered her roses,
Nourished her people,
And cleansed her hands.
But here,
He drowns my settlements,
Surges my contours,
Ruins my harvest with his acidity.
And all because
Her kiss is more intense.

Natasha Collie (17)

All My Dreams - Haikus

Sweet dreams I have dreamt,
My mind filled with clouds and smiles,
Happy all the while.

Nightmares I have had,
My mind filled with terror, gore,
Eerie opening doors . . .

Illusions I've had,
Night, after night, after night,
Always a great sight.

Natalie Tomlinson (12)

Mrs Rusk

You taught me throughout my primary seven year,
You comforted me of my high school fear,
You've supported me in all that I've done,
You've made my primary school memories fun.
You've helped every child,
That you've ever taught,
No matter if we've been wild,
It's just a special technique that you've got.
I'd like to take this time to thank you,
For all the teaching that you've done,
And to say that you're very special,
In every single way.
You brighten up the dullest day,
Like a bright sunshine ray.

Heather Shea (12)

Untitled

By the moonlit water's edge,
There stands a woman in white.
To show you and to guide you to,
The pathway through the night.

She longs to take you in her arms,
And show you all her dreams.
But you have got to find her yet,
And work out what she means.

By the moonlit water's edge,
There stands a woman in white.
Be sure you find her 'neath the mist,
Afore the sky turns light.

Hannah Hughes (15)
Ashby Grammar School, Ashby de la Zouch

My Poem

My old apple tree
All bald and bare
Standing in the garden
All the way over there.

My old apple tree
Full of bright pink blossom
Standing in the garden
Spreading it everywhere.

My old apple tree
Full of sugary fruit
Standing in the garden
Apples here and there.

My old apple tree
Red and yellow and green
Standing in the garden
Becoming bald and bare.

Daniel Lee (15)
Ashby Grammar School, Ashby de la Zouch

No Words Can Describe

Each little laugh, each little cry,
Fills your heart, the stars and sky,
Your heart was emptied but now it's filling,
For once in your life it's a new beginning.

You look for love in the world outside,
You found it but now it's died,
You got caught up in a moment so soon,
It upsets you because you thought it'd bloom.

You gave it up to save yourself,
It's time to look for someone else,
Someone else to give you love,
And to be approved from up above.

Natalie Haynes (15)
Ashby Grammar School, Ashby de la Zouch

They Laugh

They laugh
And point.
They bully me.
They don't touch
No, never touch.
But they make my life
Difficult
And miserable.

They hide my pens
They knock my stuff onto the floor
They humiliate me.
It hurts me
It burns me inside
Yet I can't do anything about it.
I never thought school
Would be like this.

Another lesson in Hell over.
The rest of the class
Rush and push out.
I look around the classroom
It's empty apart from me.
I collect my crumpled papers
From the floor.
I sit down at my desk
I plan my next lesson
And mark their homework.

Henry Hakkinen (14)
Ashby Grammar School, Ashby de la Zouch

The Day I Met You

The day I met you was a sorry day,
I remember that day like it was yesterday,
Sometimes I stop and say, 'I wish I had not been there that day,'
The warmth of your craving, the smell of your scent,
It just makes me stand and stare.

With a facial expression that would scare,
I tried to run but could not bear,
The heartache of the affair.

I remember the day I met you as if it was clear as glass,
I remember that day; we lay there on the grass,
I just stopped and stared without a care,
As my breath was taken away.

I arose from my subtle sleep
To find that you had gone
Even though I only met you once
I want you more and more . . .

The day I met you, I now regret
And wish I could forget
Erase from my memory . . .

The day I met heroin.

Liam Edwards (15)
Ashby Grammar School, Ashby de la Zouch

Untitled

She said you cared
You showed you didn't.
The years passed by
No words were shared.
I find myself standing here again
Outside your home
Outside your heart.

Lizzie Hefferin (15)
Ashby Grammar School, Ashby de la Zouch

Horse

Ten-pence, I bought you,
At a car boot sale,
That lonely look in your eyes,
The way you sat there with your body slouched
Made me want you.

Ten-pence, I bought you,
Wearied and worn.
That lonely look in your eyes,
I knew you needed a home,
That made me want you.

Ten-pence, I bought you,
I took you home.
Your eyes sparkling with delight,
But when I die,
You'll be looking for a new home.

Holly Sales (14)
Ashby Grammar School, Ashby de la Zouch

Love Or Lust

Lust is a flame from a raging fire,
Love is the embers that refuse to cool down.

Love is a carefully prepared dinner for the family,
Lust is the rubbish you put in the microwave when you're hungry.

Lust is a quick jog in the park,
Love is going to the gym three times a week.

Love is building a fence that will withstand all weather,
Lust is a fence that will stand a few weeks then break.

Lust is craving for a cigarette,
Love is going to get help to stop.

Love is something that lasts,
Lust is just desire.

Thomas Bradbury (14)
Ashby Grammar School, Ashby de la Zouch

Walking

As I walk down the garden at the old haunted hall,
Something inside me tells me I've been here before.
I can hear someone cryin' at the old haunted hall,
Something inside me tells me she's been here before.

The little girl is cryin', down by the wall,
The little girl is cryin', 'bout the old haunted hall.
Someone better tell her that the hall is no more,
Someone better tell her I've been here before.

As I look at the girl by the old haunted hall,
I realise who it is, she's been here before.
It's my cousin, who once knew the hall,
She once knew the hall when it stood tall.

Now the roofs are caving in,
And the bricks are falling out.
Now it's falling down,
Just glad I moved out.

As I walk down the garden of the old haunted hall,
Something inside tells me I've been here before.

Ben Lee (15)
Ashby Grammar School, Ashby de la Zouch

Untitled

Why does it hurt?
Why do I care?
Should I care?
Or should I not?
The pain digs deep; it's a constant ache,
Now it's all happened, I know my fate!
Thoughts and feelings move apart,
The envy, the pain, tears me in half!
Feel her feelings, think her thoughts, dream her dreams,
See an image on the wall!
It reveals the truth, don't know myself,
Who am I? What have I become?

Chris Brown (16)
Ashby Grammar School, Ashby de la Zouch

My Dog

Its dark brown eyes
Shining in comparison to his bright white fur
His short stumpy legs
Moving quickly to keep up with yours
He's like Mary's Little Lamb
Following you about.

He barks at the TV
He rips the post
He runs round when we say, 'walkies'
His tail wags almost all the time
He's happy to see us when we come in.
When someone knocks at the door, he barks for ages.

But the thing about my dog
That makes me love him
Is his human-like approach to life
He eats what we eat
He does what we do.

We call him a pet
But I call him my brother.

Matthew Dowdell
Ashby Grammar School, Ashby de la Zouch

Life

Isn't it funny how you always complain?
The way we treat you makes you insane.
You never seem to get what you crave,
Sometimes you wonder why you're alive.
And then one day your dreams come true,
That beauty you see, wants you too.
You love the way you lived before,
Everything good, knocking at your door.
Then all your dreams just fade away,
That perfect life you had goes astray.

Grace Anderson
Ashby Grammar School, Ashby de la Zouch

17

The cap's on.
The brain's gone.
Ain't got no plan,
But a big idea,
To put the world,
In the rear view mirror.

Life's a blast,
Life's a blur,
Life's short, death's better.

Engine on,
Point the GTI toward the end,
Show the world your exhaust.

Boy racer,
Boy wonder,
Boy later,
Boy under.

John Latchem (16)
Blyth Community College, Blyth

Randomness

Randomness is, the way to express.
Chickens, clouds, shoes.
The feelings that people are forced to possess.
Coffee, frogs, you.
When the world has gone insane.
Tabs, goat, this.
There's only one way to express your pain.
Life, present, death.
So use randomness, it's the only way.
Cows, grass, stars.
You say it's absurd, well here's what I say.
What . . . makes . . . sense?

Jack Clark (14)
Blyth Community College, Blyth

Tuff'un

Are you talking to me?
Moi? Ich?

No you ain't cos yer screamin'!
Screamin' an' a-shoutin'
Who the 'ell put you in charge o' us?
Yer little creep
Small'uns always 'ave to be da tuff'uns.

Na, I'm listenin' an' I'm hatin'
Da fact dat ur busy iratin'
Yer words do ma crate in
Na da 'ole room's suffocatin'
Quit yer dominatin'.

I'm hopin' an' a-wishin' yer ain't gonna say no more
Cos I'm gazin' in awe
Can't drop ma jaw!
Gotta hol' back ma beatin' heart's door.

Joanne Jones (17)
Blyth Community College, Blyth

Baby Brother Poem

When he giggles
He makes me happy
When he wiggles
He goes all wacky!

When he cries
He makes me sad
He hits me in the eye
And makes me mad!

When he's asleep
It goes all quiet
No more weep
And no more riots!

Ashleigh Humphreys (14)
Blyth Community College, Blyth

Who Knows!

She stumbles into the street.
The wind creeps up and wraps itself around her
She pulls her coat closer to her with one hand
Whilst her other hand trembles as she takes a swig from a bottle
The moonlight shines into her eyes, making them sparkle
The only source of light is the moon and it casts a shadow behind her
Her footsteps are the only thing she hears
They fade away as she turns the corner, her shadow trailing behind.
Who is she?

Her dull blue eyes search for a familiar face . . . but there isn't one
She wanders through the streams of people strolling out of nightclubs
She pushes her windswept hair out of her hair so she can see clearly
Her brown hair that's lost its shine blows freely in the wind behind her
Her eyes tell a story of sorrow
As if you can see through her soul and she's died inside
There's nothing left except the clothes she wears and the shoes
on her feet
The drunken students slide by and smile at her as if they know her
But the thing is . . . no one does.
Who is she? Who knows!

Zoe Laird (14)
Blyth Community College, Blyth

Jack The Ripper

The clock chimes one,
Night is cloaking the City of London,
Acting like a blindfold,
No sight 'til morn.

A lonesome damsel wanders the streets,
Hoping to find a one-night catch,
She pulls her shawl around her shoulders,
Tousled locks into a loose bun.

Top hat, black cloak,
A tall figure sweeps into a dark back lane,
He targets a victim,
She wanders alone, shawl wrapped around tight.

He whips out his black briefcase,
Lures the helpless prostitute to a dark spot,
With a flash of his blade,
Blood has been shed.

With a blood-curdling scream,
She falls to the ground, cold as ice,
Jack the Ripper slips back into the shadows,
A slinking, slithering snake.

Taryn Burn (14)
Blyth Community College, Blyth

The Leopard

Deep in the jungle, in the long green grass,
Lies a large spotted cat,
Resting his long, tired legs.
Then something breaks the silence,
A loud bang,
It came from the trees,
He leaps up and looks around,
They can't be far away.
He starts to run,
Bang! There it goes again,
But this time it's louder,
He grows weaker,
Then starts to slow down,
And falls to the ground
In pain.

Nicola Robinson (14)
Blyth Community College, Blyth

Adventure

In the open, doing what we please,
With all the buzzing flies and bees,
But what we do is up to us,
Go in the car or take the bus,
We could fly to our desired place,
To go to a track and watch a race,
Or go explore and find a new land,
Or a perfect island covered in sand,
Still, whatever we do is totally cool,
Jumping around or swimming in a pool,
We can do whatever we need,
Even if it makes us bleed,
All we need is a bit of strife,
To put the adventure back into life.

David Miller (14)
Blyth Community College, Blyth

A Swimming Gala

I'm standing by the pool,
It's flat, smooth and cool.
My opponents stand next to me,
Oh no, I forgot my house key.

I wiggle my little toe,
I hear the whistle go.
I dive right in,
I get stabbed by a pin.
How did that get there?
It fell out of my opponent's hair.

As I resurface,
My opponents resurface.
I'm the quicker swimmer,
Oh I want my dinner.
My arms slice through the water,
As if they were driven by a motor.
My feet are like propellers,
Everyone watching has an umbrella.

I reach the far end,
I dive, flip and bend.
I push off the wall,
I hear my mother call,
'It's almost over now,'
Tomorrow I will take a vow.
If I win,
I will ring all of my kin.
I've almost won . . .
I've won!

Michael Vallis (13)
Blyth Community College, Blyth

Fireworks Night

We are on our way,
To our fireworks celebration,
Which is just one of many,
Across our great nation.

They're all being set up now,
Hammered to the ground,
Everyone's excited,
Though not making a sound.

Here come the matches,
Which one's going to be first?
Which one is the loudest
And which one is the worst?

Bang! Goes one of them,
The rockets start screaming,
Catherine wheels are spinning,
Coloured ones are gleaming.

The Roman candles spitting,
Air bombs below,
The show has almost ended,
Crowd starting to mellow.

We leave the muddy field,
And everyone does share
The same words
'I hope it's as good next year.'

Michael Halliburton (14)
Blyth Community College, Blyth

They're Back

I hear the key
Turn in the door.
The fearsome footsteps,
The vicious voices:

They're back.

I'm not coming out from my safe haven,
Into a place of dread.
The curtain conceals me as I cower
From the unpredictable fist.

They are looking for me.

Why am I mistreated?
What have I done wrong?
Couldn't a punch bag take my place?
So I could be loved instead.

They've found me.

They tower above me,
And raise their fists.
But they will never be caught,
They will never stop.

Because all I can do is bark.

Clare Lewis (14)
Blyth Community College, Blyth

As I Walk Along

The sand feels like silk between my toes,
Tickling my feet as I walk beyond,
Crunching the stones and shattering the silence,
The sound of the ocean whistling towards me.

The sun's rays burning through my body,
Asleep in the sky on a peaceful day,
Smiling over me as I walk along,
Its open arms spread wide to greet me.

Palm trees are hunched, hiding from the world,
While the leaves whisper in the breeze,
The wind blows a tired breath,
Rustling my hair as I walk along,
Silent, wistful, singing its song.

The ocean's waves clash and bubble,
Softly swishing, silently alone,
No one's around, I'm all on my own,
But this is what I call my home.

Lynsey Fawcett (14)
Blyth Community College, Blyth

My First Love

The first time
I ever laid my eyes on you,
I knew, that you were the one,
The one for me,
The one that would make me happy.

The first time
I ever laid my eyes on you,
You left me breathless,
Every night I am sleepless,
I think of you all the time.

You are the sun that rises,
You are my tears when I am alone,
You are my life when I am gone,
You leave me breathless.

The first time
I ever laid my eyes on you,
I knew, that you were the one,
The one for me,
The one that would make me happy.

Hayley Mordue (14)
Blyth Community College, Blyth

Friends In War

In the whistling of the guns,
Feeling scared and sucking thumbs,
Waiting for my time to die,
But at that moment I began to cry.

I saw my friend and then I smiled,
But then I saw some bodies piled,
When a gun shot echoed out,
My allied friend began to shout.

My dying friend said to me,
'Be strong my friend and avenge me,'
I saw the man who killed my friend,
Then he knew it was his end.

I filled his heart with hot lead,
Then I knew it was his end,
A person behind me said to me,
'Come my friend and leave him be.'

Alex Sanderson (14)
Blyth Community College, Blyth

The Old Man!

The old man in the corner,
Sitting, staring back at me,
Someone from my past,
But his identity is a mystery.

The patch on his head,
Where the hair has disappeared,
The hair around the side,
Brings memories from the dead.

The eyes so pale and weary,
It's amazing he can see,
His face gets whiter and whiter,
With every glance at me.

But suddenly I can see,
The person who is here,
The person is my grandpops,
But my grandpops is dead!

Danielle Cunningham (14)
Blyth Community College, Blyth

I Dream

I dream of climbing in a limo,
I dream of talking to my manager Simo,
I dream of walking with two guards at my side,
I looked at my changing room as I sighed.
My name was spelt without an E,
Out of my pocket came out a key.
I dream of turning a door lock,
Opened the door, came to a shock.
My brother was there with an Avril Lavinge outfit,
I put it on as I sit.
Then he pulled out a guitar,
Walked down a corridor, couldn't be far.
Walked through the corridor onto a stage;
Played my guitar, audience in rage.
They screamed and shouted encore encore!
Then I looked down what I saw.
A guitar in my hand,
An audience, a stage, a band!

Katie Keighley (12)
Cockburn High School, Leeds

Angel Dreams

Angels sweeping across the sky
Making sure every child doesn't cry.
Dropping dreams through chimney pots
Sparkling magic dust over babies' cots.

Dreams full of happiness, laughter and fun
Of twinkling stars and a hot yellow sun.

Day trips with the family or playing outside
Feeding ducks in the park, zooming fast down the slide.

The angels are leaving, the morning has come
Goodbye to the moon and hello to the sun.

The angels fly off because their job is done
The children are up and ready for fun.

Sarah Thompson (13)
Cockburn High School, Leeds

Dreams, Dreams, Dreams

Dreams, dreams, dreams
When you go to bed you
Always dream
About something.

You think about it
When you're in bed
When will I stop dreaming?

It's like you're talking to yourself
Because nobody knows.

When you go to sleep
You dream about something
Scary or something cheerful.

It's like the dreams exchange
Or something
This time scary, this time cheerful.

When will I dream something cheerful all the time
Or something scary all the time?

If it's scary, you get scared
But when you wake up
It's just a dream!

Portia Manyemba (12)
Cockburn High School, Leeds

Nightmare

When I go to sleep at night
All I see is you
You slimy green and ugly thing
I wish you were not true
So climb into your little den
Where spiders sleep all night
Let me know just how you feel
When you are given a fright.

Jessica Barker (12)
Cockburn High School, Leeds

The Beach

On the beach I could see,
That where I was standing was near the sea.
Towards one side of the golden sands,
There were loads of people near ice cream vans.
To the right hand side of the beach, near the calm blue sea,
What I could see was a golden key.
I picked it up and walked away,
Near the dolphins that were trying to play.
I grabbed my surfboard and headed for the water,
Where a dolphin cared for her new little daughter.
I caught a wave and fell under, I couldn't see,
I fell forever and ever under the sea.
I could see a golden door and a sign pointing at me,
I knew that it was there just for me so I took out the key.
I held the key in front of the door and it went all glittery,
I placed the key in the door lock and it opened reality.

Laura Bateson (13)
Cockburn High School, Leeds

Dreams, Dreams, Dreams!

Dreams, dreams, dreams are the best
Nightmares and bad dreams I detest!
When I wake up I forget them all
But the one I remember is the best of all!
Some of my friends are in my dreams
I see them dancing whilst they clean!

Dreams, dreams, dreams are the best
They are better than all the rest!
I sometimes dream of the person I love
So when I see them I give them a hug!
I wish I could dream all day long
But whilst I sleep, I sing a song!

Cymone Rhodes & Jodie Gray (13)
Cockburn High School, Leeds

Why Do People Have Nightmares?

Why do people have nightmares?
Well, they just do!
I wonder who will be next,
It just might be you!

Why do people have nightmares?
They eat too much cheese.
Oh no, I had cheese last night,
That's why I had nightmares about peas!

Why do people have nightmares?
It could be recurring!
It could be about a tractor,
Or a house burning!

Why do people have nightmares?
They might give them a fright.
Monsters, ghosts, ghouls and vampires . . .
Will you get one tonight?

Sonya Kumar Bansal (12)
Cockburn High School, Leeds

Dreams!

Monsters crying, shouting
Playing, dancing, laughing
Real stuff,
Pretend stuff,
You could be driving in a bus
Or down in the sea
Up high in the sky
Or buzzing like a bee . . .
A dream can be extraordinary
A dream can be really scary
But just think
Do you think sleep would be the same without dreams?

Shahira Shabir (12)
Cockburn High School, Leeds

My Dream

Dreams can be good, dreams can be bad
Sometimes they make me very sad
Thoughts twirling around in my head
All this happening while I'm tucked up in bed.

Running through the pouring rain
I looked around, it was there again
The wood was dark, the wood was green
The very strange object looked very mean.

Would it get me, would I escape?
The clock was ticking, it was getting late
I hid behind a tall, broad tree
I want to be away from here, I want to be free.

Just as I think, *will this nightmare ever end?*
Approaching from the distance, I see my best friend
All at once, my fear disappears
As the bright morning sun suddenly appears.

Haley Lapping (12)
Cockburn High School, Leeds

Dreams

Dreams are so frightening
Dreams make me scream
The way they haunt me all through the night
My dreams are sometimes nice
When I dream of things like small little mice
I scream, I shout, I roll about; I jump up for the light
The night is dark, the street lamps are bright
The way they shine all night long
The light was bright that it gave me a fright
Everyone was sleeping but I was still dreaming
It came to the morning and everyone was yawning
After a good night's sleep
Dreams, dreams, plenty of dreams.

Dawn Wager (13)
Cockburn High School, Leeds

Dreams

On the way to the supermarket
When a man comes along
He asks for a bit of food
So I give him some and walk away.

Down the path
Coming up was a lovely sun
Beautiful, but then the day got colder,
My mood changed, it was dark.
There was a castle in front of me.
I walk into the old, abandoned building,
It is cold and scary
Cold shivers up my back.

All the rooms are empty . . .
But there are ghosts - everywhere!

I am running, running out into the light
I awake, it was a dream . . .

Drifting away to sleep . . .

Christopher Moseley (12)
Cockburn High School, Leeds

My Dreams

My dreams are scary, my dreams are wild
I like dreams nearly all the time
I love dreams about football when it's me against the world
With my family in the background watching me score some goals
In the end I wake up, it's all just a dream
Until the next night . . .
When I can have the dream again.

Thomas Young (12)
Cockburn High School, Leeds

Dreams

Dreams, I love dreams
Until one day I wished
I would never dream again.
In my dream
I saw my favourite pop star
Being taken away from me.
The only way to
Get him back from
That evil woman was . . .
To travel on a thin
Rope and rescue him
From the wicked woman.
As I travelled down
This rope I reached
Him and I tried to
Grab him, the wicked
Woman chopped off
My hand and I
Fell in the deep
Dark hole and I
Lost my favourite pop star.
When I woke up
My ankle was bruised
It seemed I was
Sleepwalking and
The black hole was
My dustbin in the corner.

Angel Muketu (13)
Cockburn High School, Leeds

Flower Power

Roses are red
Violets are blue
I had a dream
And I thought of you.

Buttercups are gold
Daisies are white
In my dream
You were a beautiful sight.

Bushes are green
Tree barks are brown
In my dream
You wore a crown.

Sunflowers are orange
Poppies are pink
In my dream
You were so stunning I couldn't think.

Christopher Page (12)
Cockburn High School, Leeds

My Dream About My Friendship

I had a dream
It was about a girl,
She was a nice girl,
And she said to me,
'Friendship is like glass,
When it's broken, it will never mend,
Friendship is like glue
You have always stuck with me
Nobody can split us up.'

Lauren Tate (12)
Cockburn High School, Leeds

Dream

One night I was dreaming
The stars were gleaming
Then I started screaming
Where was I?

Lying in my bed
All this happening in my head
I'm scared and frightened, full of dread
Why?

I toss, I turn, I scream, I shout
Lots of scary things about
Someone please help me out
Will they?

The sun rises, dazzling and bright
Drawing an end to my dreams and fright
I hope I sleep better tonight
Will I?

Charlotte Lapping (12)
Cockburn High School, Leeds

I Dream

I dream of a place of peace and no hunger.
I dream of a place of feeling and wonder.
I dream of a voice calling to me.
I dream of many wonders, wow, but why me?
Even though these things may not have effect,
I still know they're there
Waiting to come out and connect.

Yasmin Rhodes (12)
Cockburn High School, Leeds

A Dream

A dream is like
Your own life story
When you snuggle up in bed
With Ted the bear all snuggled up too
All cosy and warm
Your dream walks into your room
As quiet as it can be
Actually, it's just like you and me
With eyes, a nose, ears
And maybe arms and legs as well.

Some of them cry
Some of them lie
Some of them smile
Some of them even take you down the aisle.

So listen up close
And take a pose
'Cause a dream
Could be after you.

Tanjila Begum (12)
Cockburn High School, Leeds

Scary Stuff

Some dreams are scary
And give me frights.
When people are murdered,
In the middle of the night.
They walk round streets
Holding a very sharp knife.
I just wish they would go away,
And never come back at night.

Jordan Graham (12)
Cockburn High School, Leeds

I Had A Dream!

I had a dream to live my life in peace.
But the monsters you see would not let me be.
They stalked me at night, as I shivered in my bed.
They gave me a fright, and they hid in my shed.
But what was I to do, I had no other choice.
At twelve, my age, my friend had a ghost.
But this was much worse . . . at the very most.
So I'd try to go to sleep, I tossed and I turned.
My bed light still glowing, it burned and burned.
Then it hit me, quite hard . . . if only I could see.
These ghosts of mine are just like me.
They walk and they talk, they laugh and they play.
They always lurk and hide in the day.
When my mother died, they came to me.
To scare me perhaps or maybe to help me.
I'd have done it all before, when I was younger, nearly four.
But back then my mum would just close the door.
Send them away forever, until the day my mind flies away.
From goblins and ghouls . . . but wait! They've gone.
My ghosts at last, are a thing of the past.
My dream is nothing except a stream of consciousness.
Only I have the power to control what I see.
Come with me, flow down my stream
And see my adventures from one of my dreams.

Aimee McVittie (13)
Cockburn High School, Leeds

Nightmares

Monsters chase me when I'm asleep.
When they chase me I begin to weep.
I hear them getting closer in the night.
I know if I see them they'll give me a fright.
They're about to get me, so I scream, then I wake up . . .
And it's only a *dream!*

Shaun Emmett (12)
Cockburn High School, Leeds

My Dream

My dream is hard to say
I can't find the way.
My dream was of a man walking down the street
He was in a car; black and green
He was chasing after me.
I was scared but then my dream
Was chasing after me!
Then there was a voice saying 'a dream, a dream was after me
And this is why I flee, I flee.'
This dream.
The dream appears to be very happy with me.
Then I wake up; it's morning
I can't wait till night again
When my dream comes true.

Megan Davidson (12)
Cockburn High School, Leeds

The Monster And I

Once I dreamed of a monster
The monster's face was red.
There was water on the floor
Water on its head.

I thought I'd seen it before
Then it started to scream
And then I realised that
This person wasn't just in my dream.

I then knew who it was
It was none other than the evil . . .
Six-year-old . . . *my brother!*

Thomas Sampson (12)
Cockburn High School, Leeds

Dreams To The End

Dreams can always soon come true
At the end of the day, it's down to you.
Nightmares all come soon to an end
But dreams keep going and make amends.
Life is hard but life is great
My heart and my dreams decide my fate.

So keep on dreaming, don't be blue
Don't let the nightmares get to you.
What do dreams make you feel?
They make me feel so happy and real.
So follow your dreams right to the end
'Cause when you get there, there will be your best friend!

Georgia Wilson (13)
Cockburn High School, Leeds

Eagles

The golden eagle is a bird of prey, the giant osprey too,
But there's one more majestic than the both of you.
It lays its eggs in abandoned nests, where others used to be,
On mountain ledge, above the trees where it can be free.

She soars high and low across the countryside,
And as the day wears on she sees a hare and begins to dive.
Down, down, down she goes at speed of a colossal rate,
Nearing the ground with outstretched claws, the hare has met its fate.
Away she flies with outstretched wings, across the tops of trees,
Till she reaches home again to eat and rest in peace.

Emma Cariss (13)
Cockburn High School, Leeds

Daydreams

When I daydream
It's never an appropriate time
In maths or science, or English or art
Whether it's at school where the teachers are shouting
Or at home where your mother is talking
It's never an appropriate time!

Daydreams are crazy, funny or scary
Daydreams are weird or stupid
They could be about monsters or giants
Or they could be about family or friends
Whatever the daydream, dream it quick
Before you get yourself into trouble!

Samantha Pickles (13)
Cockburn High School, Leeds

Dreams And Nightmares

A dream, on my face puts a gleam
But nightmares are so mean.

When I have a dream
It makes me beam.

When I have a nightmare
I get the sudden scare.

But, my dear
A nightmare is nothing to fear.

A dream is ace
Something to put a smile upon your face!

Dale Beck (11)
Cockburn High School, Leeds

Song

A noise can change the world,
As the plucked cat gut throbs,
A child has a comfort,
The wailing infant's scream,
Becomes melodic.

Rapture begs for song,
A joy beckons for a voice,
To herald it.
The laughter - a brilliant fanfare,
To announce the arrival of triumph,
And rejoice.

As the grief washes in,
Requiem rings out.
The tears a hushed lullaby,
To sooth and inspire,
A renaissance.

Song, sweet song,
Which stands the test,
The bold innovators,
Who never ever regurgitated.
Music, sweet music,
Wished by so many to caress,
Always there,
Yet untameable, ungraspable . . .

Alison Tod (16)
Craigmount High School, Edinburgh

Love I Found In You

You are the air I need to breathe
The river of life inside of me.
You are the half that made me whole
You are the anchor of my soul.

And you are strong when I am weak
You are the words when I can't speak.
You never fail to see me through
That's the love I found in you.

You are my shelter from the storm
You are the road that leads me home.
Baby, with you here, face to face
Oh, I know I found my place.

'Cause you are strong when I am weak
You are the words when I can't speak.
You never fail to see me through
That's the love I found in you.

Once in every life
You find the one who's right.
And when you say forever, it's true
That's the love I found in you.

You are strong when I am weak
You are the words when I can't speak.
You never fail to see me through
That's the love I found in you.
That's the love, love I found in you.

Toofel Babar
Crown Hills Community College, Leicester

My Favourite Person

(Based on 'Sonnet 18' by Shakespeare)

'Shall I compare thee to a summer's day?
Thou art more lovely and more temperate,
Rough winds so shake the darling buds of May
And summer's leave has all too short a date!'

Shall I compare you to a delicious iced cream bun?
You're extremely loving and sharing
Let the lightning fall upon me but I know
You are there just like the sun
But most of all, you're always caring!

Shall I compare you to a beautiful butterfly?
Always soft-hearted you are
Never say bye
Always big-hearted you are!

Nusrat Patel
Crown Hills Community College, Leicester

My Mother

My mother is sweet as a strawberry.
Her eyes are always sparkling like the stars.
My mother is as kind as an angel.
Her voice is lovely like the ocean.
When she taps on my back, all my worries are gone.
When she shouts at me, it sounds like she doesn't really meant it.
She is special to me.
Better than ever.

Kajal Peshavaria
Crown Hills Community College, Leicester

The Greatest Man

There is no man dearer to me,
Throughout the whole of history.
Then the one who was sent as a guide,
Leading people from darkness to light.

How I wish my ears could hear,
The greatest teacher to ever appear.
As he sat with his companions so dear,
Beautifully preaching with love and fear.

How I wish my heart to emulate,
The greatest man that my Lord did ever create.
As he did demolish vice and hate,
As his kindness did reverberate.

How I wish my character to be,
Like the purest of mankind undoubtedly.
He who played with children lovingly,
He who was rarely seen unsmilingly.

How I wish for such determination,
As him - the greatest illumination.
The truth he conveyed to the entire nation,
As he guided them with his motivation.

Never could the sun outshine,
This beautiful prophet of mine.
How I wish to be like he,
The noble prophet Mohammed, upon him may peace be.

Mubeen Hafeji (14)
Crown Hills Community College, Leicester

My Mother

She's so tender,
Her face with a glow from the sun.
She's so slender,
Her hair as dark as the night sky.
A heart of gold with a sprinkle of diamonds.
Her advice like God's word.
She's so truthful,
Her green eyes are like emeralds.
She's so helpful,
Her lips are as red as rubies.
Her hand on my shoulder whisks all my worries away.
Her praise takes me over the moon .
She's so understanding,
Her soul as precious as a pearl.
She's so soothing,
An aroma of lavender around her.

Fatima Mullaji
Crown Hills Community College, Leicester

Untitled

M y father is my favourite person for many reasons
Y ears of happiness I hope we have.

F orever we all will be together
A dmire him because of what he has done for me
T hankful for all his help taking me to sports
H onesty is his asset
E ntertaining he is, all the jokes he makes
R igorous in competitions.

Wasim Majid
Crown Hills Community College, Leicester

Volunteer

The metal slams
Cutting and biting
Its teeth gnaw at the earth
Savaging the delicate roots
Slicing vital stems.
The spade's withdrawn
Only to slam down
Again and again.
Sweat drips in the summer sun
As he hacks at the plant
Begrudgingly, it loosens
Ripping and tearing
He strikes at the next.
The hack and slash
The sweep and clear
The stagnant water's lazy smell
Bites into his weakened mind
Numbing.
The long and pointless repetition
Over and over and over
Again
And again
But there's no end in sight.
He stares hatefully into the muddy depths
He can never finish
There is always more.
He puts down the tools
And glances left then right
The chains on his weary ankles clatter
The murky water takes him.

Ed Salkeld (17)
Downfield Sixth Form

Sleeper

I know what I am
Cast aside and looked down upon
Spat at from a distance
Tell me I'm wrong

If you could just hate me
At least then I'd exist
Even if it's at a distance
I don't want to be dismissed

I've learned I mean nothing
I exist outside what's real
The pain you cast upon me
I guess time doesn't heal

And when the bell finally tolls
And they tell you that I've died
At least I'll know the church was empty
At least I'll know no one cried

Where are your insults now?

Tom Newman (17)
Downfield Sixth Form

Silence

Swans glide
Through the silken blue river
Into sunset
Fish follow in the dream-like state
Of the imagination

Wind caresses
Hills and valleys

The river weaves silently
Through the green pastures

The spring bubbles up from below
In the cool, dark ground

It is daybreak
Life exists

Panpipes awake us from the silence
Calm never ceases to exist.

Charlotte Carter-Jones (17)
Downfield Sixth Form

Dereliction

Dark, dank dampness nestles
In crevices, cracks, creeping and oozing,
Pushing the peeling paint apart.
Splinters and fragments of glass litter the carpet, smashed,
From the shattered panes, leaving jagged,
Jutting teeth in the doors,
As an immense mouth
Gaping into the cavernous darkness
Of the garden beyond.
Shafts of moonlight illuminate
The cobwebs that ache to be hidden.
Unveiled, they shine silver
In the moonlight,
Pearly silver droplets suspended
On shimmering silver strands.

Dexter Stevens (13)
Downfield Sixth Form

Dad's Secret

Sometimes you have to tell the truth,
You don't know who it will affect,
Dad's behaviour was very uncouth,
Not just his family he had wrecked,
Ricky Prescott was full of proof,
It's truth he needed to protect,
His family ended up in tears,
Because of him and his cashiers.

Fiona Bailey (13)
English Martyrs Catholic School, Leicester

Smile!

Now I've left you for a while,
Do not cry - stand up and smile,
Laugh and joke and play and love,
I'm smiling at you from above.

You stand at my grave and still look down,
Don't you know I'm all around?
So smile and laugh, please don't weep,
I didn't really fall asleep.

I'll never leave, I'll never fade,
I'm in this paradise God has made,
So do not cry and grieve for me,
I'm going to safely, RIP.

Don't forget the good times we had,
I can't stand it when you feel so sad,
Do not sit in silent prayer,
I'm still here - I'm everywhere.

Come on, smile, it's not the end,
You know that one day God will send
His angels, to come and bring you too,
And we'll smile together - me and you.

Rebecca Whitmore (14)
English Martyrs Catholic School, Leicester

Poverty

There once was a boy called Clement
And this boy was reasonably poor.
No one ever realised what he meant
Him and his friend went singing door to door.
He received the message that I sent
But he didn't need money anymore.
He said he had resorted to stealing
I had no idea what he was feeling.

Louise O'Connor (14)
English Martyrs Catholic School, Leicester

I Would Put In My Box . . .

(Based on 'Magic Box' by Kit Wright)

I would put in my box . . .
The love and fun times from my family and friends,
The gossip and secrets that would never end,
The delectable dessert named strawberries and cream
And the happiness from all my dreams

I would put in my box . . .
The achievements I received at home and at school,
The pepperoni pizza that always made me drool
My magical memories from the past
And the phone calls to my friends which always last.

I would put in my box . . .
All of my favourite treats and chocolates,
The pictures I took of my mates,
The TV programmes I could never switch off
And the small and pleasant scents that make me cough.
These are what I would put in my box!

Karen Tew (12)
English Martyrs Catholic School, Leicester

Untitled

(Based on 'Magic Box' by Kit Wright)

I would put in my box
A photo of my family and friends
'Cause I know they will be there forever.

I would put in my box
A photo of the shining sun
To show the days full of fun.

I would put in my box
Drawings of art which I thought were cool
Which had been drawn in the school
And, if I could, I would put a star in my box
To show the nights, with the stars so bright.

Charlotte Dixon (14)
English Martyrs Catholic School, Leicester

I Would Put In My Box . . .

(Based on 'Magic Box' by Kit Wright)

I would put in my box . . .
The roar of football fans scoring at the World Cup final,
The fantastic footie that brightens my day,
The crazy cartoons I spend hours watching,
The DVDs that make me doze away.

I would put in my box . . .
The amazing Arsenal winning the Premiership,
The magnificent music that drifts me into a world of my own,
The sound of cars crashing and bullets blasting on my XBox,
My glittering guitar that I strum silently on.

I would put in my box . . .
The sticky, slimy sweets that I munch on,
The creamy chocolate that I stuff myself on all day,
My enthusiastic Easter with chocolate eggs galore,
Scary school after the holidays long but now gone.

I would put in my box . . .
The happiness of my friends, family and pets,
Wonderful Winnie, Splendid Spice, Horrendous Hagrid
The comfy coat of linen I wrap myself in at night,
The slippery snowmen disintegrating in sun, bright.

Alasdair Farrell (12)
English Martyrs Catholic School, Leicester

God's Box

I want to make a box
Sort of like what God gave to Pandora,
I won't give it to Fort Knox
I won't give it to my sis Laura.
To go into this box is pain and suffering
The feeling of anger and hatred,
I shall make it out of God's power
So never shall this box be opened.

Christopher Tennant (14)
English Martyrs Catholic School, Leicester

I Would Put In My Box . . .

(Based on 'Magic Box' by Kit Wright)

I would put in my box my funny, fantastic family and friends,
A friendship that never ends,
A creamy, crunchy, caramel chocolate bar,
A fast and furious racing car
And my blue, bouncing, bouncy ball.

I would put in my box a cold and creamy ice cream,
My favourite, fantastic football team,
My clever, clumsy, cuddly cat,
My big, black, basketball hat
And my perfect, priceless PlayStation 2.

I would put in my box my lovely and large TV,
A comical comedy DVD,
My soft, silky, super chair,
My terrifically tidy, teddy bear
And my crazy, complicated, colourful computer.

I would put in my box a large, great, green Christmas tree,
The booming, buzzing sounds of bumblebees,
My comfy, cosy, clean bed,
My thin tennis racket, rather red
And a long-lasting laughter that lasts forever.

Benjamin Chung (11)
English Martyrs Catholic School, Leicester

Bullying

My friend was getting bullied, he was in pain
I felt something bubbling up, it was anger
The truth though, it was all a big frame
I wished I could get him with a dagger
My friend did cry because he was in shame
Then I felt like I was in big danger
My very high popularity died
I wanted to walk home, and go and hide.

Josh Murphy (14)
English Martyrs Catholic School, Leicester

I Would Put In My Box . . .

(Based on 'Magic Box' by Kit Wright)

I would put in my box . . .
My blue bedroom,
My gossiping, giggling girlfriends,
The fruity smell of sloppy, slushy strawberries,
My favourite fab stash of music CDs,
And the marvellous smell of Maccy D'S.

I would put in my box . . .
My fabulous family and friends so I could keep them forever and ever,
Also the sound of love, laughter and joy,
And going into town to meet the brave, bold boys.

I would put in my box . . .
The taste of icy ice cream,
And the feel of the ice cream trickling down my throat.
I like going to classy cinema shows,
And wearing my cool, casual clothes as they flow.

Charlotte Coulson (14)
English Martyrs Catholic School, Leicester

I Will Put In

(Based on 'Magic Box' by Kit Wright)

I will put in my box the look on my mum's face on my first birthday
And when I nearly burnt the house down on Christmas Day.

I will put in my box the cool feeling on a summer's day
And the feeling when I jumped in a freezing pool.

I will also put in the box the taste of creamy, caramel chocolate
And the juicy taste of fried French fries.

I will put in my box all my childhood memories
And store them safe for the future.

Riya Chauhan (14)
English Martyrs Catholic School, Leicester

What Is It That I See?

I can feel it moving
In-between my toes,
I can smell the air
Through my nose
What is it that I see?

I can see little creatures
Weaving in and out
I can touch the mist
Which is scattered about
What is it that I see?

I can taste the rain
Pouring down on me
I can feel the heat
My family and me
What is it that I see?

As I walk along
I reach somewhere
I take a look
But I do not dare
What is it that I see?

I walk up a hill
And what do I see?
I walk up more
I feel like a bee
What is it that I see?

I shall tell you no more
I shall tell you no less
I shall give you no clues
Not in distress.

I am at the seaside!

Alexandra Males (12)
English Martyrs Catholic School, Leicester

Summer

I love summer
Everyone is cheerful
I play in the park
And am not fearful.

The grass is lush green
Flowers are blooming
Everyone is smiling
Instead of fuming.

Holidays are great
The sea laps the shore
Sand is glistening
And the seagulls soar.

Stay in a big tent
Or a caravan
Pack your summer stuff
And then go get a tan.

August is brilliant
Very hot and sunny
Water fights in the garden
Everyone finds funny.

The end of summer
The days are shorter
The nights are longer
And we drink less water.

Rebecca Cross (12)
English Martyrs Catholic School, Leicester

The Witching Hour

Witching hour comes once a year,
When children are full of fear,
When they're tucked up in bed with fright,
Witching hour is tonight!

It is midnight, so get into the light,
Before you get a fright,
At witching hour!

So off to bed with fears and tears,
Watch out for your wardrobe my dears,
For no it's not the bogeyman's sight,
No, it's witching hour tonight!

It's midnight,
So get out the light,
Before you get a fright,
At witching hour.

You're alone with no sound,
You can hear your heart pound,
To your room they'll fly from the great tower
So get ready for witching hour!

Shannon Carroll (12)
English Martyrs Catholic School, Leicester

Lauren's Poem

So many Africans in desperate need,
Every three seconds a child will be dead,
AIDS is spreading to the kids that they breed,
All this suffering when you are in bed,
You think you're in pain if you're cut and bleed,
When they're starving, it makes me see red,
Why it hasn't stopped is a mystery,
Please help us make poverty history.

Lauren Moore (14)
English Martyrs Catholic School, Leicester

Untitled

(Based on 'Magic Box' by Kit Wright)

In my box I will place . . .
My seaside sun
My enthusiastic experiences
My fantastic fun
And my loyal religion.

In my box I will place . . .
My fluorescent football
My great goals
My treacherous tackles as I fall
And my ballistic boots.

In my box I will place . . .
My family and friends
My cocky cousins
My loyal lends
And my gifted grandparents.

In my box I will place . . .
My dopey drawings
My colourful crayons
But colouring is boring
Still, I like my fantastic felts.

This is what I would put in my box
Plus my grand games
My extravagant XBox
My willing, wireless controllers
Well this is what I would put in my box!

Darragh Holloway (12)
English Martyrs Catholic School, Leicester

I Would Put In My Box

(Based on 'Magic Box' by Kit Wright)

I would put in my box,
My fabulous family and friends,
The loving laughter of my family that never ends.

I would put in my box,
The sound of my jingling jewels,
And the excitement of splashing in swimming pools.

I would put in my box,
My cosy, comfy, cream chair,
And my timid teddy bear.

I would put in my box,
The sweet taste of succulent strawberries,
And the taste of chilling cherries.

Laura Foley (11)
English Martyrs Catholic School, Leicester

Friends

Friends are like flowers
They cheer us up when we're down
And give us special powers.

Friends cheer us up
They make us laugh when we're sad
They bring us great luck.

Friends give us advice
Most of the time it is good
Friends are very nice.

Friends help us succeed
So we can do great things
What more do we need?

Holly Hughes (12)
English Martyrs Catholic School, Leicester

I Would Put In My Box . . .

(Based on 'Magic Box' by Kit Wright)

I would put in my box.
The cheer of my fun friends
And give them cool, creamy chocolate that I would send
My comfy, cosy chair
And sit on it with my tiny teddy bear.

I would put in my box
Things I shouldn't show
Because if I did, I'd gleamingly glow
The nice, sunny summer's day
And call for my friends so I could play.

I would put in my box
The last, huge, heavy thing I had
And leave everything that made me mad
The long-lost love of my life
And ask my gorgeous girlfriend to be my wife.

Paul Smith
English Martyrs Catholic School, Leicester

The Tables Have Turned

I am the one who was battered and bruised,
I was used as a punchbag for you to be amused,
I am the owner of the clothes you pinched,
You kicked me and hurt me but I never flinched.

My dinner money was taken, every last pence,
I had to fetch your ball when it went over the fence,
You hit me when I didn't do what you say,
You killed my dog to make me pay.

Now the tables have turned,
And I am one of the popular folk,
But, forever, my heart will be broke.

Toni Crook (14)
English Martyrs Catholic School, Leicester

I Would Put In My Box

(Based on 'Magic Box by Kit Wright)

In my box I would put . . .
A spurt of stimulation
The inspiration of imagination
The succulent silence of a sanctuary
The heavenly taste of peaches and berry.

In my box I would put . . .
The warmth of my home
The freedom and fun of being alone
The peace of a church
The exciting exhilaration of a wondrous search.

In my box I would put . . .
The love of my life
A cuddly, cute cat
My uncle's dead wife
My very best hat.

I would put in my box . . .
A fragile, fresh fountain
The love of my family
The will to climb a mountain
And sweet, secure success.

Carly Griffiths (12)
English Martyrs Catholic School, Leicester

Bullying

At first I thought they were messing around
I don't know why they're doing this to me
But it's just too much, I can't stand my ground
And how is it fun? I really don't see!
Why they hate me so, I really don't know
Why do they do this? It is so wrong
Why do those cowards think they are on top?
All of this bullying, it should just *stop!*

Naomi Pinchbeck (14)
English Martyrs Catholic School, Leicester

I Would Put In My Box . . .

(Based on 'Magic Box' by Kit Wright)

I would put in my box
All my fabulous family and friends
A lovely life that never ends,
My tiny teddy from childhood
A £1 screwball would be good.

I would put in my box
Lots of love,
The sweet lullabies my mum loved,
All the times I've played the keyboard
And all the delightful days I was never bored.

I would put in my box
The sweet-smelling air of winter days,
All the times the cuckoo clock plays,
The crackling of the fire when it's cold,
With the marvellous crackling coal.

I would put in my box
The first fish I ever caught,
And the first toy I ever bought,
All the cool Christmases I've ever had,
Listening to melodic music that makes me glad.

James Nelson (12)
English Martyrs Catholic School, Leicester

Ella's Fear

Ella was crippled in terrible fear
And she was definitely very scared
The price for her life might be very dear
But try and run away, she hadn't dared
Ella felt Fin was now quite close and near
Feeling very restless, her soul she bared
Having been hurt, she had been beaten
Ella had not drunk, she hadn't eaten.

Joel Carton (13)
English Martyrs Catholic School, Leicester

I Will Put In My Box . . .

(Based on 'Magic Box' by Kit Wright)

I will put in my box,
The sweet smell of fragrant fresh air,
The shimmering shine of the summer sun,
The soft, silky feel of newly washed hair,
And the enthusiastic excitement of kids having fun.

I will put in my box,
The taste of melted, magnificent chocolate cake,
Loads of squidgy, sugary sweets,
The sun bouncing off a luscious lake,
And my favourite music's bashful beat.

I will put in my box,
A soft, squishy sofa with a matching chair,
The giggly, girly sleepovers with my best friends,
The soft snugly feel of a teddy bear,
And everybody's everlasting life, that never ends.

Harriet Lee (11)
English Martyrs Catholic School, Leicester

What Is It Like To Be Hated?

My heart bleeds and nobody knows
So this is how my poem goes
I wish I wasn't created
That's what it's like to be hated.

Pretending like you really care
But all you did was sit and stare
I feel like I'm always gated
That's what it's like to be hated.

I'll say goodbye cos I'm going
As I don't think this is flowing
When we spoke we still debated
That's what it's like to be hated.

Rebecca Sweeney & Paris Connolly (12)
English Martyrs Catholic School, Leicester

I Would Put In My Box

(Based on 'Magic Box' by Kit Wright)

I would put in my box . . .
Me and my friend's dance,
In the fragrant flowers
The hot, sweet scent of popcorn.

I would put in my box . . .
My colourful, purple room that shines in the sun,
Hot Sunday dinner on a warm afternoon
A white icing cake that I call a bun.

I would put in my box . . .
The feel of the cool, calm pool that glistens
The ice-cold ice cream shivering down my spine,
Seeing a cat born, three little kittens
That's what I would put in my box!

Irainna Marraffa (12)
English Martyrs Catholic School, Leicester

I Would Put In My Box

(Based on 'Magic Box' by Kit Wright)

I would put in my box . . .
My lovely friends' laughter all around,
My favourite food and a barking sound,
A nice pleasant picture of my friend,
A pair of trainers, the latest trend.

My favourite book and a fan,
My picture I took of my tan,
A handful of Haribo sweets,
A memory of frostbitten feet.

My tremendous TV,
My sunny RV,
A convertible car,
A painful picture of my ma.

David Preston
English Martyrs Catholic School, Leicester

I Would Put In My Box

(Based on 'Magic Box' by Kit Wright)

I would put in my box . . .
The cool, calming fresh sea air,
The gorgeous, glossy shine on wet hair,
The silky soft fur on newborn kittens,
The comfy cuddle of hand-knitted mittens.

I would put in my box . . .
The gleaming glow when you win a race,
The small, sweet smile on a baby's face,
The shining sun setting over a tropical sea,
The fuzzy-feeling hug from someone that loves me.

I would put in my box . . .
The terrific taste of strawberries and cream,
The almost awake feeling after a dream,
A child's surprised smile on Christmas morning,
Listening to an old man's stories that are brilliant yet boring.

Alicyja Uczniak (12)
English Martyrs Catholic School, Leicester

Ella

My life could not get any worse
I am affected by a curse
My life is just so very sad
If only things were not this bad.

Most may love me, someone hates me
Why is my life not so easy?
My family are very mad
If only things were not this bad.

I wish that life would just go back
When raging storms came to attack
To be back home, I'm very glad
If only things were not this bad.

Jessica Morgan (13)
English Martyrs Catholic School, Leicester

I Would Put In My Box

(Based on 'Magic Box' by Kit Wright)

I would put in my box . . .
My fun family and foolish friends,
The feel-good feeling of Fridays,
And the brilliant, binding force of BMX biking.

I would put in my box . . .
The technique and tactics of tennis,
The soft squeaks of my guinea pigs,
The dashing beauty of Daisy my dog,
And the carnivorous feeling of chips and cod.

I would put in my box . . .
The icy intent of ice cream,
While watching a funny film,
The foul fumes of ferrets,
And the awful aroma of faggots.

I would put in my box . . .
The trashy TV on a Saturday night,
The fantastic feeling of watching a big fight,
The heavenly feeling of holidays,
And the burning amount of chillies in a hot curry.

Edward Rees (12)
English Martyrs Catholic School, Leicester

Why Do I Feel Like This?

Why do I feel like this, tired and afraid?
Many people think I am very troubled,
Doing nothing on my bed I laid,
Ella was missing, I was crumbled,
I was frightened and started to fade,
The last moments, I was fumbled,
Inside my heart was totally bare,
But I knew that she was in a lair.

James Westhead (13)
English Martyrs Catholic School, Leicester

I Would Put In My Box

(Based on 'Magic Box' by Kit Wright)

I would put in my box . . .
My groovy gentle gran
My delightful, dopey dog chasing after the postman
My fashionable fantastic friends.

I would put in my box . . .
My tasty apple pies
My passionate pepperoni pizza that I baked
My fantastic French fries
My crazy, cheeky chocolate cake.

I would put in my box . . .
My bulky birds that fly in the sky
The cuddly cats that jump so high
The devoted dolphins that jump and leap
The terrific tigers that would be so hard to keep!

I would put in my box . . .
The tall, trembling trees that cover the land
The roaring rivers that slide over the sand
The hills that touch the sky.

I would put in my box . . .
The fantastic football matches
The critical cricket that lasts so long
The busy basketball games
The rattling rugby games which are top notch
And that's what I'll put in my box!

Brooke Manion (12)
English Martyrs Catholic School, Leicester

I Would Put In My Box . . .

(Based on 'Magic Box' by Kit Wright)

In my box I would put . . .
The electric emissions of my guitar
A super-fast Ferrari as my car
My Woodgate shirt with number eight on the back
A Man U shirt with wonder kid Wayne on the back.

In my box I would put . . .
The love and laughter from Mum and Dad
My super-fun friends that are really glad
When I jump for joy, when it's my birthday
And a relatives reunion when it's Christmas Day.

In my box I would put . . .
The trashy TV shows
A real cool film that flows and flows
The most creamy chocolates and sweets
And funky flavours of ice cream that I would like to meet.

Ciaran Campbell (12)
English Martyrs Catholic School, Leicester

All On My Own - Kyrielle

Im all alone, no one is here
Someone please come as I'm in fear
I really wish, I could have known
Here I am, sitting on my own.

I'm missing Mum and missing Dad
I wish they were here, I feel sad
I could ring, if I had a phone
Here I am, sitting on my own.

With my family I felt so well
Why did you do this, please just tell?
I wish I was not all alone
Here I am, sitting on my own.

Nicola Rodrigues (13)
English Martyrs Catholic School, Leicester

I Would Put In My Box

(Based on 'Magic Box' by Kit Wright)

I would put in my box . . .
My comfortable and casual everyday clothes,
My funny and funky friends from school,
My melodic music that my brother loathes,
My blue and silver bike that I ride on - it's cool.

I would put in my box . . .
The crunchy and crispy sensation of chicken dippers,
The funky and pleasant photographs that I keep in my room,
My dad's breakfast; killer smell of kippers
Late at night, looking up at the sky, seeing the stars and the moon.

I would put in my box . . .
The memories of my brilliant and bubbly brother,
My big and bouncy bed that I sleep in at night,
My marvellous and mischievous mother,
The ray of sunshine that comes into my window all bright.

Lauren Cotton (12)
English Martyrs Catholic School, Leicester

Ella - Kyrielle

I used to go out all the time,
Back then, that was before the crime,
I had a happy family,
Until he came and kidnapped me.

Kind of weird Sam had always been,
With his friend who was never seen,
But Sam was so normal you see,
Until he came and kidnapped me.

It was my fate, I had to die,
All because of my father's lie,
I was the shy girl, that was me,
Until he came and kidnapped me.

Rachel Meehan (13)
English Martyrs Catholic School, Leicester

A Hand In The Mist

Lara walks in the woods
With her faithful dog Spot
Over the dark slushy mud
Through the darkness they trot.

Lara is scared! She's lost her way
Spot spots something in the mist
The pair will get a fright this day
As a deformed grey hand ventures in the mist.

Spot barks but is silenced
As a creature with a howl appears
And before Lara has turned, the monster has pounced
She looks up and fright becomes tears.

Spot lies on the floor, stomach open
The creature looks up, needing to be fed
Lara knows it's a werewolf there and then
She knows also she will soon be dead.

The monster leaps, ready to kill
Lara defends herself, only with her hands
Pain is coming, ready to fill
The werewolf only nips then stands.

The wolf then sprints back into black
Lara drops to sleep in the cold night air
She awakens in morning with a chill down her back
The urge of flesh fills her fangs and grey, bristled hair!

Ryan Ashenhurst (12)
English Martyrs Catholic School, Leicester

Confused - Kyrielle

She came along all on her own,
I followed her, I liked her tone,
I just wish that Ella was near,
Why has she gone, why is he here?

She looked like Ella, gave me hope,
But it turned out to be a joke,
To think of Ella brings a tear,
Why has she gone, why is he here?

I hear the man in the wheelchair,
Could this just be a big nightmare?
I wish things in my mind were clear,
Why has she gone, why is he here?

Kidnapper could have taken me,
But I was hidden then you see,
I sat inside, in so much fear,
Why has she gone, why is he here?

Rosin Shearer (13)
English Martyrs Catholic School, Leicester

Cornered, Helpless

Cornered, helpless, I am being trapped
I feel like a wronged victim now beaten
Troubled, bewildered, I have been kidnapped
Famished, starved, I have not drunk or eaten
I'm also persistently being slapped
All of this nonsense is for no reason
I will find a way out of here, I am scared
For all of this trash I was unprepared.

James Baines (13)
English Martyrs Catholic School, Leicester

I'm A Young Kid, No More Than Three - Kyrielle

I went at night to chase the storm
The golden girl made me feel warm
I nearly fell into the sea
I'm a young kid, no more than three.

There was a girl and she was nice
She smelt pretty, a lot like spice
She always had a lot of glee
I'm a young kid, no more than three.

Then she went, she left me alone
A strange man then rang on the phone
She's left me now, someone help me
I'm a young kid, no more than three.

In the darkness I lie awake
For the sound of laughter she'll make
My dad is bad, he is naughty
I'm a young kid, no more than three.

Niall Williams Gordon (13)
English Martyrs Catholic School, Leicester

Secrets

He didn't tell me, now I'm furious
I used to love him but now I feel hate
Are there more things now I am curious?
He says he is sorry but it is too late
Nobody tells me, I feel glorious
We are now enemies, he was my mate
I cannot believe it, I am so shocked
The door to the awful secrets is locked.

Rebecca Mundin (13)
English Martyrs Catholic School, Leicester

Tsunami

I've got a tale to tell
From not long ago,
It's about a tsunami
Full of sadness and woe.

It struck unexpected
Nobody knew,
There weren't many survivors
Only a few.

It smashed through families
And tore them apart,
It broke many things
No doubt someone's heart.

It hit the news
Like lightning to metal,
People falling apart
Like flowers - petal by petal.

And even when it's over
It sure left its mark,
And it won't leave minds
Whether it's light or dark.

Lucy Godsmark (12)
Guide Post Middle School, Choppington

Help!

As I sleep there is no sound at all
Then I am awakened by Captain's call.

It's terrifying when you hear a crash
It's frightening when you see a flash.
'Guns at the ready,' I hear the sergeant call
We trudge through mud trying not to fall.

Anger and hatred fill the soldiers' eyes
As gas is released, I hear the sorrow and cries.

Linzi Ibbetson (13)
Guide Post Middle School, Choppington

This Love Is . . .

This love is unbreakable,
It's unmistakable,
Every time I see your face,
My heart starts to race.

This love is so blinding,
I feel your love winding,
And winding through me,
'Cause I love ya, you see.

This love is our thing,
It makes my heart sing,
Each time I look into your eyes,
I know why.

This love is unbreakable,
This love is untouchable,
This love is *ours.*

Stephanie Sweet-Burton (13)
Guide Post Middle School, Choppington

Love Poem Dear . . .

You are a well fit lad,
And your body's really not that bad.
I really, really love you so,
And if you ask me out, I won't say no.
I don't care where we dine,
Just let me be your valentine.
I love your laugh and your smile,
I'd like to stay with you a while.
You're the object of my desire,
Deep inside you light my fire.
I long to see your smiling face,
Floating through the cyberspace.

Alice Nicholson (13)
Guide Post Middle School, Choppington

Have What You Want

Have a tree, that's big and brown
Have a hyena, with a big, funny frown!
Have a flower with no colour,
Or run faster with a marathon runner.

Laugh your head off to a clown's dance
Or lose yourself in a Derren Brown trance.
Ask a homeless man how much he has,
Or ask him if he's cleaner than Fairy or Daz?

Be as dumb as Scooby-Doo,
Or be Peter Andre, doo-doo-da-du-doo.
Be as insane as you want,
Cos the council will want more warrant.

Be a great rapper like Eminem,
And climb a tree higher than Big Ben.
Try your hardest all your soul,
As long as you don't end up in a deep black hole!

Jamie Lee Irving (13)
Guide Post Middle School, Choppington

Mustard Gas

'Mustard gas! Mustard gas! Quick, on your knees!'
The Germans firing explosive shells, causes us to flee
Wherever you go it seems to follow
Running from the mustard gas that I'm about to swallow
Scrambling through the trampled flowers
Repeating this hour after hour
Trying to fit the clumsy masks
'Help me! Help me!' the young boys ask
And this is what I came here for
Seeking fame and fortune galore
When I arrived, I knew I was wrong
All because of those mustard gas bombs.

Thomas Davison (13)
Guide Post Middle School, Choppington

How Many Bodies Will Lie?

I stand, fighting for my country
With a knife, stabbing bluntly
My friends are dying
The services were lying
This is not good
People shed blood
Dying for your country
Like a knife stabbing bluntly.

'Tis a sin not to fight
You can die, lose your sight
What's so great about fighting?
I would rather be writing
My parents worry:
'What will happen to our sonny?'
Then there were shouts of Sergeant Byers
'Men, hold your fire!
They are members of our team!'
But, too late, they all scream
What have we done?
This war's no fun!
We've killed our men
How many left, fifteen, ten?
How many more will die?
How many bodies will lie?

Fighting for your country
Like a knife stabbing bluntly
How many soldiers will die?
How many bodies will lie?

Louise McLeod (13)
Guide Post Middle School, Choppington

War Poem

Bombs drop, shells smash
Guns fire, tanks crash.

As men prepare
I wonder, do I dare?
The signal goes, my heart starts to beat
Suddenly I feel the heat
Tanks follow and fire
I feel like my life is going to expire
As I fight for my country
My soul grows hungry
I want to go home
I feel so alone.

Suddenly, a scream, 'Gas! Gas!'

Men start to worry
I reach for my mask in a hurry
Men that are late
Know their fate
Men have cried
But now they have died
Men have fought for their lives
But in return, got stabbed with knives
No more begging on our knees
As we remember with poppies.

Bombs drop, shells smash,
Guns fire, tanks crash.

Natalie Hodgson (13)
Guide Post Middle School, Choppington

Seven Ages

(Inspired by 'As You Like It' by Shakespeare)

All the world's a football pitch
And all the people score a goal
They have their weaknesses and strengths
Their job is to score the ages of man.

At first, the infant
Desperately trying to walk and crawl.
And then the schoolboy
With his football boots and shinpads and kit
Trying to score a goal.
And then the lover
Trying to be a professional footballer
And trying to impress his girlfriend.
Then the footballer
Trying not to let the goal past
Willing to try and make his team win
And to win the League.
And the manager
Trying to get the best team
And trying to win every cup
And to get the best trainer to train his team.
The sixth age is
Winning all the cups
And getting all the best players
Going into retirement.
And at last, the old man
Sitting in his house, struggling to do anything
Remembering all the good times in his life.

Ryan Eadington (11)
Guide Post Middle School, Choppington

Do You Love Me?

I will shelter you on stormy days!
When we travel, I will help you on the way.
Do you love me?

If you are tired, I will clean for you.
If you are stuck, I will help you through.
Do you love me?

If you need a cuddle, you can ask me.
If you are cold, I'll fetch you a cup of tea.
Do you love me?

If something is on your mind, come and tell me.
If you get locked out, I will give you a key.
Do you love me?

I will be your doctor and help you when you're hurt.
I will clean you if you're covered in dirt.
Do you love me?

If we were a pair of birds, we would be doves.
If I was Cupid, I'd make us fall in love.
Do you love me?

Kayleigh Smith (13)
Guide Post Middle School, Choppington

Love

Love is like a bubble,
Sometimes it causes trouble.
It sticks on your mind;
Especially when it's kind.
Sometimes it brings joy;
Other times it causes pain.
Love is like a big red pool
Of hugs, kisses and thoughts.
Love is a subject
That cannot be taught.

Emily Straughan (13)
Guide Post Middle School, Choppington

Christmas Poem

I hang out my stocking,
At this time of year.
What pressies could I get,
A bike or a teddy bear?

You're wrapping up presents,
For your daughter or son,
You're getting ready,
For some festive fun.

The time is now,
The time is here,
Everyone's full
Of festive cheer.

Have a great time
In every way,
Have fun
On Christmas Day.

John Blaney (12)
Guide Post Middle School, Choppington

The Ring Of Fire

Love is a burning flame,
And it can turn into a fiery ring.
I fell into a burning ring of fire,
When we met you became my one true desire -
The ring of fire, the ring of fire.

This fiery ring will bring me closer to you,
You're just like a perfect fitting shoe.
For love is a brilliant thing,
When it makes a massive, fiery ring.

All I want is for you to be with me,
Don't make me kneel down and start to plead.
Just be my valentine,
In the ring of fire.

Marc Merrilees (13)
Guide Post Middle School, Choppington

Cupid's Drawn Us Together

Cupid's drawn us together
I'll love you whatever the weather.
Roses and flowers I don't need
I don't even care if all I get is a weed.
I just want you with me forever
I don't want to let you go - not ever.
All I want is you in my arms and never to let go
Just don't ever leave me, please no!

I want you to be mine
And if you say yes, let's celebrate and bring out the wine!
So let me be your valentine
You're always on my mind.
So I guess all that means - I love you.

Natalie Cockburn (13)
Guide Post Middle School, Choppington

The Haunted Kitchen

At the sink
The taps were running
Like a nose
With a cold.
The great big
Sunken eyes
Of the double sink
Stared hard.
The chair turned its
Single, cushioned eye at me.
It stood for about fifteen seconds
Then came charging after me
It kicked me with its thin wooden legs!

Paul Charlton (12)
Guide Post Middle School, Choppington

A Spell Poem

(Inspired by 'Macbeth')

Hubble bubble toil and trouble
Insects burn and cauldron bubble.

Spot of ladybird, whole load of bugs
Shell of snail and antennae of slugs.
Swarm of ants, body of insects
The wing of fly creating lots of effect.
Body of woodlouse, legs of a spider
The eyes of the caterpillar go in, growing wider.

Hubble bubble toil and trouble
Insects burn and cauldron bubble.

Fur of dog and tail of cat
Tongue of frog and wing of bat.
Skin of snake and big eyes of owl
Eye of newt and lion's growl.
Ear of elephant, neck of giraffe
As the ingredients go in the witches laugh.

Hubble bubble toil and trouble
Insects burn and cauldron bubble.

Christina Brophy-Rowell (11)
Guide Post Middle School, Choppington

The Haunted Kitchen

The dishwasher smashes the plates
The oven burns the cakes
The washing machine chews the clothes
The sink turns its trunk - tap and squirts water.

The chair runs around
Its big eye chair - back glowing
The table rolls towards me
The pouffe jumps on the spot.

Fiona Gray (11)
Guide Post Middle School, Choppington

Word Party!

Talented words sing and dance
Lucky words take a chance.
Crazy words are totally mad
Unhappy words are very sad.
Snobby words have their nose in the air
Nasty words pull your hair.
Wealthy words get lots of pay
Lazy words droop all day.
Brainy words read a book
Sly words pry and look.
Scary words alarm and shock
Pretty words wear nice frocks.
Friendly words love and care
Kind words are polite and share.
Athletic words leap and soar
Greedy words always want more.
Careless words trip and slip
Naughty words pinch and nip.
Exciting words never bore
Sleepy words like to snore!

Georgia Reay (12)
Guide Post Middle School, Choppington

The Haunted Kitchen

Sink, drip, drip dripping with evil eyes.
Dishwasher opens its mouth
To show sharp, knife-like teeth
The washer creeps up on me
To eat up my clothes.

The chair moved its evil cushion eye
Stood still for two minutes
Then galloped towards me
Then took its best shot and
Kicked me with its wooden legs!

Katie Drysdale (11)
Guide Post Middle School, Choppington

A Spell To Banish School
(Inspired by 'Macbeth')

Double, double, boil and bubble
Wand turn and school muddle.

The ink of a Parker pen
In the cauldron at the den.
Nose of dog, ear of boy
Eye of girl, piece of toy.
Microchip, CD Rom
Teacher's foot, toe of Tom.
For a spell to banish school
Like a pot full of gruel.

Double, double, boil and bubble
Wand turn and school muddle.

Dictionaries off the shelf
In the pot with an elf.
Pinch of salt, a garden pea
A bit of sugar and a flea.

PC monitor and a book
Eye of bat and point of hook
For a spell of magnificent trouble
Like a stew, spoil and bubble.

Double, double, boil and bubble
Wand turn and school muddle!

Paul Marshall (12)
Guide Post Middle School, Choppington

Haunted Kitchen

The growling washing machine blinks its red eyes,
Glows and throws clothes.
Sucks you down its big round throat.
Red eyes shining on the moonlight,
Dials ticking, ready to attack.

Liam Traba (12)
Guide Post Middle School, Choppington

The Teacher Spell

Teachers, teachers go away,
Never come back any day.
The suck of a little leech,
Let the teachers never teach.
Take all of the sums out of maths,
We'll place the teachers in cold baths.
Put the teacher on a stake,
Then watch them burn, boil and bake.
Take the grease of a dirty creature,
Put it in the mouth of a teacher.

Teachers, teachers go away,
Never come back any day.
Put the teacher's eye in a broth,
Watch the children cackle and cough.
Tail of newt and toe of dog,
Flush the teachers down the school bog.
Steal the smell of a scruffy dog,
Turn the teachers into a frog.
Pinch the spot off a witch's nose,
Push the teachers into a hose.

Teachers, teachers go away,
Never come back any day.

Megan Dryden (12)
Guide Post Middle School, Choppington

Haunted House

Spitting chicken nuggets at me
The oven's red devil's eyes
Stare in the moonlight.
The timer makes the bleep of death
Its gleaming teeth snarling at me in hatred.
The greasy oven door talking to me
Telling me I will die
Its lips curling as if it's going to eat me.

Levi Ford (11)
Guide Post Middle School, Choppington

Word Party

Scary words frighten other guests
Clever words give each other tests.
Silly words pull funny faces
Fast words have running races.
Lazy words sit down on a chair
Fighting words pull each other's hair.
Funky words dance and sway
Athletic words jump and play.
Romantic words call each other honey
Rich words give each other money.
Gloomy words mope around
Quiet words don't make a sound.
Violent words start many fights
Energetic words stay up all night.
Sad words always cry
Going words say goodbye.
Happy words like to smile
Tidy words clean and file.
Hurt words rub their cuts
Hungry words eat all the nuts!

Alex Guy (13)
Guide Post Middle School, Choppington

Haunted Kitchen

The oven growled at me.
A chicken shot out
Like a bomb
From a sauna.

The dishwasher crackled
And banged.
The plates smashed
Like a mouthful
Of broken teeth.

Chris Johnson (12)
Guide Post Middle School, Choppington

The Word Party!

Jiving words like to jump and jive
Hip hop words like to dance and perform live.
Tango words like to step and whirl
Waltzing words like to twirl and twirl.
Ballet words like to spin and leap
Unprofessional words end up in a heap.
Pop words shout and dance
Salsa words like to show off and prance.
Line dancing words dance in a line
Tap-dancing words point their toes fine.
Classical words like to go with the flow
Jazzy words like to sparkle and glow.
Raving words jump up loud
Rock words like to sing with the crowd.
Foxtrot words like to trot and trample
Pink words like to rage and ramble.
Disco words move with the beat
R'n'B words like to dance in the street.
Charleston words like to kick and pounce
But all of these words like to dance and dance!

Hannah Scott (13)
Guide Post Middle School, Choppington

Haunted Kitchen

The oven door
Growled like a tiger
Its devil eyes
Lit up like a fire
It wobbled towards me
Ready to bite
Its chattering mouth
To gobble me up!

Andrew McLennan (11)
Guide Post Middle School, Choppington

Word Party

Funny words make you smile
Athletic words run a mile.
Wriggling words worm away
Time words pass the day.
Lazy words slouch and sit
Empty words describing it.
Musical words create a tune
Silly words make a loon.
Movement words chug along
Bustling words make cities throng.
Serious words, stern and grim
Dark words make rooms dim.
Stupid words, brainless and dull
Angry words fight like a bull.
Adhesive words stick together
Light words describe a feather.
Dialogue words sweetly chat
Domestic words, dog and cat.
These are our words, there are so many
Make us a book called a dictionary.

Liam Hunter (13)
Guide Post Middle School, Choppington

Haunted Kitchen

The fridge door opened
The light came on.
It screamed, shouted
'Stay away from me!
I am a big monster
With big sharp teeth
I have a watery tongue
And I eat children!'

Daniel Halley (12)
Guide Post Middle School, Choppington

Word Party

Happy words give a smile
Athletic words run a mile.
Lazy words sit all day
New words come out in May.
Scary words scream and shout
Hyper words run about.

Artistic words make pots from clay
Restful words sleep all day.
Sad words weep and cry
Clever words wear a tie.
Strong words lift up weights
Funny words get lots of mates.
Mathematic words draw lots of charts
Mechanical words fix up parts.
Performing words shout on stage
Aggressive words are shut in a cage.
Sneezing words go atishoo!
Miming words are just like you!

Mario Coxon (13)
Guide Post Middle School, Choppington

The Attic

Voices whisper
Rusty pipes slither, their mouths gargling
Funeral suits unfold
Embarrassing stories keep their mouths shut
In the corner spiders' victims buzz
Singing jewellery boxes record another song
The floorboards creak
Woodlice emerge
Ornaments clank together
Photographs keep their smile in place
Uniforms camouflage with dust and dirt
The bright green grass
Sunbathing out in front of the crumbling house.

Hannah Connolly (12)
Guide Post Middle School, Choppington

Ancient Attic

Dust gathering on a bundle of lice.
Bones of animals turning to ash.
Bags of cement questioning and calling.
Outrageous furniture yelling.
Cables coiling, hissing and hanging.
Boxes of nails, old and rusty.
Aged cobwebs hanging angrily.
Bluebottles suffering in silence.
Frozen pipes screeching, squawking.
Cracked floors wailing.
Bricks silently gazing.
Newspapers telling of ancient stories.
Rolled-up carpets like lollipop sticks.
Magazines crackling and coughing.

Samantha Burns (12)
Guide Post Middle School, Choppington

The Attic

Powdery bricks crumble,
Cracked wash basins grumble,
Old crisp packets rustle,
Hovering hosepipes hang,
Dusty floorboards creak,
Rotten planks lean against a wall as cold as stone,
The stench of sewage fills the air,
Bags of cement cough grey smoke,
Twittering woodlice scuttle,
Thick cobwebs tear,
Broken sideboards sleep,
Tearful windows shatter,
Broken bones lie in a jar, staring.

Fatimah Shafiq (12)
Guide Post Middle School, Choppington

Word Party

Funny words laugh and giggle
Wormy words squeeze and squiggle.
Scary words scream and shout
Lively words jump about.
Hungry words devour and take
Artistic words sculpt and make.
Musical words play a tune
Summer words come out in June.
Relaxing words sit and laze
Dreamy words sleep and doze.
Fumbled words are mixed and confused
Second words are old and used.
Adhesive words stick together
Permanent words are there forever.
Little words are small and tiny
Metal words are hard and shiny.
Aggressive words argue and fight
Nocturnal words come out at night.
Equivalent words are the same as each other
Rivalling words hate each other.

Sam Haswell (13)
Guide Post Middle School, Choppington

The Garage Poem

Broken washbasins bellow,
Cobwebs rip,
Rolls of rope hang disgracefully,
The sagging roof wails,
Ancient doors whisper,
Woodlice scamper from the light,
Hosepipes lie across roof beams like coiled up snakes,
Rotten deckchairs hide silently,
Dead bluebottles lie in their battlefield,
The squeaking of a mouse breaks the silence of the garage.

Anthony Gates (12)
Guide Post Middle School, Choppington

The Word Party

Happy words laugh and smile
Sad words are now worthwhile.
Funny words are comic and witty
Mad words are angry and gritty.
Embarrassed words are flustered and red
Shy words are never said!
Selfish words are mean and greedy
Kind words help out the needy.
Active words go out for a run
Lazy words laze about in the sun.
Boyish words play out in the mud
Girlish words are very good!
Colourful words make pretty drawings
Dull words are very boring.
English words eat bacon and eggs
French words feast on frogs' legs!
Black words are dark like night
White words are ghosts that give me a fright!
All words help me write and speak
No words make life very bleak!

Kay Shiel (13)
Guide Post Middle School, Choppington

The Creepy Garage

In the dusty, swaying garage rubbish flutters
Great rotting crates stare at scurrying rats below
Swaying walls crumble under the sagging roof
Rolls of cable hang like sleeping snakes
Bags of cement lean over the damp, rotting floor
Dusty jars of dancing bones
Great boxes of dirty, rusting nails clatter
Heaps of clattering brass pipes chatter
Old, cracked washbasins gurgle dust
Piles of old deckchairs sit and rot.

Josh Kelly (12)
Guide Post Middle School, Choppington

The Word Party

Climbing words jump and leap
Water words swim to the deep.
Lazy words fall to the ground
Money words get a penny to the pound.
Fit words go to the gym
Bright words are never dim.
Sporty words could run all day
Quiet words have nothing to say.
Smart words admire Einstein
Scary words admire Frankenstein.
Simile words are as cool as can be
Sailor words are proud at sea.
Comfy words just relax
Sharp words are like an axe.
Smelly words are sometimes nice
Curry words go well with rice.
Wrestling words are very gruff
Violent words are very rough.
Hair words love the comb
Poetic words wrote this poem.

Andrew Thompson (13)
Guide Post Middle School, Choppington

Attic

As I shuffled through the attic door,
Hosepipes swung to and fro,
Under the dust, dead bluebottles, buried,
Opening the chest, woodlice scurried,
Old newspaper scrunched up tight,
Spiders scattered in the torch's beaming light,
Dust fell from everywhere,
Cobwebs stuck to my hair.

Nataliya Forster (12)
Guide Post Middle School, Choppington

Five Stages Of Frank Lampard

(Inspired by 'As You Like It' by Shakespeare)

All the world's a footie pitch
Players brawling and bowing
He has the exits and entrances
His acts being five stages
At first, the infant
With his football
Crying and crawling . . .
And then the Youth Training Scheme
Shooting and scoring
Celebrating and shouting . . .
Then the lover
Leaping and laughing
On the level . . .
Now the signature
Chelsea signing
And Chelsea singing
Then playing for Chelsea
Chelsea celebrating and being crowned
Premiership champions!

Jamie Young (12)
Guide Post Middle School, Choppington

The Garage

Rain dives from above,
Woodlice march,
Rats scurry,
Hosepipes droop like slithering snakes
Stacked up boxes like drooping palm trees,
Spiders stalk
Newspapers shuffle
Bones rustle
The floor lets out a quiet moan,
Half-eaten bluebottles dangle from webs.

Nathan Anderson (12)
Guide Post Middle School, Choppington

The Word Party

Crazy words dance on the moon
Silly words get drunk in the Toon.

Boring words send me to sleep
Scary words go around and creep.

Dancing words get down tonight
Moving words jump in the light.

Wet words end up in puddle
Long words get in a muddle.

Funny words make you laugh
Dirty words have a bath.

Angry words shout and scream
Sewing words mend a seam.

School words are full of books
Model words care about their looks.

Writing words use a Parker pen
Nice words are good friends.

Big words go in the ring to fight
Little words are so light.

James Gray (13)
Guide Post Middle School, Choppington

In The Garage

Pipes rattle,
Rolled-up carpets flinch,
Old chests of drawers crumble,
Kit bags full of England rugby kit,
Hosepipes roll by with their hands in their pockets,
Bluebottles prey,
Spiders pounce,
Kitchen units crouch,
Woodlice crawl along the floor like army tanks,
Ropes shake like trees in the wind.

Chris Smiles (12)
Guide Post Middle School, Choppington

The Garage

Wind shakes garage
Roof looms overhead
Threatening
Severed carpets splay,
Rubbish slow-dances across the floor
In the corner
Ancient kitchen units creak
Like soldiers in the forest
Mice attack
The sink gurgles
Chainsaw roars
Boxes flinch
Cages swallow butchered toys,
Cables whip from the wall
Ropes have frayed ends,
Birds lay stone-dead.

David McClenn (12)
Guide Post Middle School, Choppington

I Just Wanna Be Yours

(Inspired by 'I Wanna Be Yours' by John Cooper Clarke)

Let me be your Lamborghini
I'll drive you anywhere.
You can wear a pink bikini
On the beach with flair.
I will love you day and night
I won't let you out of my sight.
Let me be your big bright star
I'll buy you chocolate from the Spar!
Let me be your brand new kitten
I will tease you with my paws.
Let me be all these things
'Cause I just wanna be yours!

Craig Sanderson (13)
Guide Post Middle School, Choppington

All The World's A Stage

(Based on 'As You Like It' by Shakespeare)

'All the world's a stage
And all the men and women merely players
They have their exits and their entrances.'
In her life she plays lots of characters
Her acts have been seven stages in life.
At first the baby
Crying in the mother's arms.
And then the bored schoolgirl
With her handbag and school books
Always demanding money.
Next, the flirting teenager
On the hunt for boys
Showing 100% attitude.
Along comes university, getting a career and becoming an adult.
Soon the job, working hard for money
She cannot go to Mam or Dad anymore
It's a hard life.
Now it's time to retire
Getting wiser by the minute
Spending a lot of time in the kitchen
And being a taxi driver.
Here's the finale
The last stage in life
Losing teeth, losing taste, in fact, losing everything.

Jordan Hogg (12)
Guide Post Middle School, Choppington

A Spell To Make The School Vanish

(Inspired by 'Macbeth')

Trouble, trouble, and more trouble
You will be gone within these bubbles.

Voices of the teachers shout
Vanish within the cauldron's cout.

Pieces of paper, bits of string,
Blades of scissors, a sticky thing.

Breaktime bell and playtime clatter,
Lunchtime noises, chatter, chatter.

Silly English, boring maths,
Dinner ladies, insulting staff.

Trouble, trouble and more trouble,
You will be gone within these bubbles.

With Mr Thouret's pots of paint,
In the cauldron you're a saint.

After school, detention's bad,
Take eye of man and ear of lad.

Ink of pen and lead of pencils,
ICT and plastic stencil.

For a spell to make some rubble,
Mix carefully, watch it bubble.

Trouble, trouble and more trouble
You will be gone within these bubbles.

Thomas Reid (12)
Guide Post Middle School, Choppington

The Furniture Game

In a tall tree,
I am a coconut with a hard, brown shell and lots of hairs
I'm President Bush
An old American treated like royalty
At the top of Mount Everest
In the white snow, cold as ice
I'm quick to snap
A Venus flytrap
Catching flies
With my bones like a suit of armour
And a rock-hard exterior
I am the armadillo.

Dark as blood
And the colour of love
I'm the colour red
Tall and sharp
Viewing the world
I'm the Empire State Building
The third planet
A Martian landscape
A huge red planet
Living in the town
I'm a Geordie
I'm the soft caramel and fudge bar
You can't resist
I'm a Mars bar.

Wayne Almond (12)
Guide Post Middle School, Choppington

Spell For Horror

(Inspired by 'Macbeth')

Tumble, tumble, in a jumble,
Find some animals in the jungle.
Lizard's leg and wing of bat,
Fish's fin and claw of rat.
Snail's shell and paw of bears,
Dog's eye and ear of hare.
Lobster's tooth and skin of jowl,
Crab's claw and talon of owl.
Turtle's head and leg of frog,
Leopard's spots and nose of hog.
Tumble, tumble in a jumble,
Find some animals in the jungle.
Bird's legs and heart of mouse,
Dragon's breath and foot of louse.
Tiger's stripes and beak of gull,
Dolphin's tail and horn of bull.
Lice's teeth and head of pig,
Dalmatian's dots and snout of earwig.
Butterfly's body and colour of greenfly
Pheasant's feathers and nail of magpie.
Tumble, tumble in a jumble,
Find some animals in the jungle.

Laura Yule (12)
Guide Post Middle School, Choppington

The Spell On How To Make Your School Fall Down

(Inspired by 'Macbeth')

Double, double, boil and bubble,
Turn this school into a pile of rubble.
Pages of books, claws of hens,
Sweaty trainers, ballpoint pens.
Brain of a teacher, tail of a dog,
Empty files, croak of a frog.
Squeaky chalk, ear of a pig,
A classroom clock, actor's wig.
Double, double, boil and bubble,
Turn this school into a pile of rubble.
Dictionaries, classroom lights,
Pencil cases, girls' tights.
Classroom blinds, dandelion weed,
Pupils' hair, loads I need!
Jug of water, skipping rope,
Homework diary, no homework I hope!
Bottle of vinegar, bubbling froth,
Now I have finished my brilliant broth . . .
Double, double boil and bubble,
Turn this school into a pile of rubble!

Jessica Storey (12)
Guide Post Middle School, Choppington

In The Garage

In the dark and gloomy garage . . .
Wood rots and nails trundle.
Timer stands as still as the rotting old wall.
The sagging roof frowns.
Bags of rubbish rustle.
Ropes hang from nails like sleeping snakes.
Hosepipes stare.
Newspapers whisper about the past.
Bags of cement grow as still as rocks.
Pots of bones rattle.
Dust floats down to the ground like a parachute.
Spiderwebs catch flies in mid-air.
Woodlice scurry into dark corners.
Windows creak.
Kit bags swing like monkeys.
Books flick their pages.
Papers dance across the floor.
Old carpets, rolled up, play host to slugs and beetles.
Old heaters snarl, old drawers slam shut to hide their secrets.
But I still feel that there is something else there.

Connor Bye (12)
Guide Post Middle School, Choppington

Dark Is . . .

Being alone in a haunted house
A black shadow on the floor, moving
Being killed in the dark
Black cats in the spooky dark
Thunder and lightning in the night sky
A dark haunted school
A really black school jumper.

Nadine Williams (12)
Hartridge High School, Newport

The Eyes Of The China Dolls

Fear is china dolls. . .
I lay in my bed,
My eyes getting used to the dark,
And I see them.
They stand there and stare.
I blink, open my eyes wide,
And they're still there.
They seem to move.
They know I'm here.
I just wish they'd disappear.
Their unblinking eyes seem to say,
'We're here, we're watching
And we're here to stay!'
There's so many of them,
And only one of me.
I put them there.
Two, twenty-four, thirty-three.
As sleep takes hold,
My duvet is my den.
I think about my night-time starers
Who in the daytime are my friends!

Amber Flynn (12)
Hartridge High School, Newport

Fear Is . . .

Spiders' fangs.
Snakes slithering in front of me.
Having a tooth taken out.
Ghosts flying through the house.
Vicious dogs chasing you.
Scary high places because you think you're going to fall off.

Mark Sutton (11)
Hartridge High School, Newport

Fear Is . . .

Fear is . . .
Spiders with long legs.
Going to the dentist to have a tooth taken out.
Heights like being on a mountain.
Bees when they sting me.
Death, when people in my family die.
China dolls when they stare at you all day.

Richard Timbrell (12)
Hartridge High School, Newport

Dark Is . . .

Dark is . . .
A bottomless chasm.
The look of my evil brother.
The shadow of night.
The robe of the Grim Reaper.
The cloak of a vampire.

Carl Jones (11)
Hartridge High School, Newport

Fear Is . . .

Big, smelly feet.
Being high above the floor.
Green runny snot.
Big red eyes.
Seeing dead, smelly animals.
Having a tooth pulled out at the dentist.

James Bristow (12)
Hartridge High School, Newport

Dark Is . . .

A black cat with dark glowing eyes.
The very bottom of the ocean.
The dark colour of my uniform.
An empty tunnel with no light.
My black school shoes.
When you're driving down a lane at night.

Danielle Young (12)
Hartridge High School, Newport

Dark Is . . .

A school jumper.
Night-time.
Shadows in the night.
A black cloud.
An empty house.
A black chair.
When the light is turned off.

Bethan Wilkins (12)
Hartridge High School, Newport

Dark Is . . .

A big black cat.
A long tunnel.
My school shoes.
A school jumper.
A clear blackboard before work.
A black car.

Preston Killoran (12)
Hartridge High School, Newport

Fear Is . . .

Fear is . . .
A dark forest
With a shadow in the distance.
That's fear.

Falling down a well
And not being able to get out.
That's fear.

A room full of snakes
But no door to get out.
That's fear.

Being in a plane crash
In the middle of nowhere.
That's fear.

Aliens invading Earth
To take over mankind.
That's fear.

Writing a poem
For someone to read.
That's my biggest fear.

Jamie Watkins (11)
Hartridge High School, Newport

Some Animals Are . . .

Some animals are fierce,
Some animals are gentle,
Some animals are large,
Some animals are small,
Some animals are fast as the wind,
Some animals are as slow as a flower growing . . .

Riah Goodison (13)
Hartridge High School, Newport

Fear is . . .

Bugs, they come out when it rains
Dark, it really scares me
Feet, they all stink of cheese
That's what really scares me!

Fairies, angels I like most
But when ghosts go, *'Boo!'*
That's what scares me most!

The witch is really scary
Her name is Scary Mary
But when she takes
Her mask off
She is really, really scary!

Chelsea Sims (12)
Hartridge High School, Newport

Dear Leah

You are always in my heart,
Those nasty rumours tried to break us apart.
You are a great sister,
Even though sometimes you were like a painful blister.
I can't wait until we meet again,
I can't live with this terrible pain.
The prison is a terrible place . . .
I can't wait until I see your face.
In my heart is where I keep a friend,
Our love will never end.
I can't wait until you come home,
Love you, little bro.

Kieran Pugsley (13)
Hartridge High School, Newport

Fear Is . . .

The sound of the screams when waiting in the dentist.
The heights below the cliffs.
The flights above the clouds.
Creepy spiders when it is dark.
Bright and bold fiery sparks.
Bugs that crawl all over you.
Clowns that jump around shouting and screaming, *'Boo!'*
Hot-house fires and big loud explosions.
Going up hills in cars in case the brakes don't work.
Fears of frowns, I don't like seeing people down!

Abbie Selkirk (12)
Hartridge High School, Newport

Fear Is . . .

Fear is watching a scary movie on my own.
Fear is walking on the edge of something very high.
Fear is when a dog runs at you with its teeth out.
Fear is a car coming right at you, fast.
Fear is your first time flying on a huge aeroplane.
Fear is paragliding through the air like a bird.
Fear is a man with a gun taking an innocent life.

Tace Ahern (12)
Hartridge High School, Newport

Fear Is . . .

Fear is watching a horror film in the cinema.
Fear is someone scared of heights and stood on top of a cliff
or bridge.
Fear is being followed or thinking you are being followed.
Fear is fearing something that isn't there . . .

Daniel McKinley (14)
Hartridge High School, Newport

Fear Is . . .

Creepy-crawly spiders and fierce masked riders.
Freaky clowns and dribbling hounds.
Dreadful heights and tiny mites.
Heavy dark and brown bark.
Creaking doors and squeaking floorboards.
Being home alone and going in a dome.

Big dark monsters.
Small gooey spaces in unpredictable cases.
Catchable illnesses and nasty misses.
Mean, nasty teachers and scary preachers.
Blood-sucking leeches and loud screeches.
Buzzing bees and biting fleas.
These all petrify me . . .

Amy Vrettos (12)
Hartridge High School, Newport

Fear Is . . .

Fear is . . .
Spiders crawling along my ceiling.
Worms slithering along my carpet.
Moths zooming around in the air.
Needles digging into me when they're not meant to be there.
Daddy-long-legs scaring me, making me run away.
Bumblebees chasing me, trying to sting me.
Posters staring at me every time I make a move.
Smelly feet stinking the whole house down.
Green bogey frightening me,
I'm thinking it's going to flick at me.
Red eyes staring angrily at me.

Helena Ali (12)
Hartridge High School, Newport

Fear Is . . .

Spiders big and black and hairy
Crawling all around, oooh, scary!

Bloody-thirsty zombies all around
Rising up from underground.

Locked in a coffin underground
No one can hear you, not a sound.

Teachers and learning
The teachers shouting, 'Grammar!'
And leaving you squirming.
And fear is . . .
Clowns, alone in their funhouses, waiting to pounce!
Aaah!

David McFadyen (12)
Hartridge High School, Newport

Dark Is . . .

Dark is . . .
My black school uniform, dull and plain.
Shadow darting across the room.
My shoes in the hot sun.
Being alone in the dark and frightened.
Dark is an empty pit when I die.

April Glue (12)
Hartridge High School, Newport

Dark Is . . .

A computer screen when it is turned off.
My bedroom when my curtains are closed.
A shadow flying across the room.
A black bag in the bin.
A black cat at night with yellow eyes.
The night sky when there are no stars.

Jade Sutton (12)
Hartridge High School, Newport

Fear Is . . .

My fears are . . .
Ugly feet that come out in the sun.
Bees that are buzzy and buzz.
Spiders with crawly, furry legs.
China dolls that stare when you walk away.
Rats with long, thin tails.
Thunder when it cracks.
Lightning when it flashes.
People when they bang their teeth together.
Slugs that slither around your garden.
Snakes curled up in their cages.

Emily Drave (12)
Hartridge High School, Newport

Fear Is . . .

Fear is . . .
People wearing sandals in the summer.
Waiting to have teeth out in the dentist.
Seeing spiders on the floor.
Walking through the woods in the dark.
Stepping on slimy slugs.
Being on top of a high building.

Kirsten Williams (12)
Hartridge High School, Newport

Fear Is . . .

The dentist's - waiting for a filling.
The sound of a snail's shell crushing.
A house with no lights on.
An empty house with no one in.
Seeing a ghost in my bedroom.
Sleeping on your own.

Becky Lloyd
Hartridge High School, Newport

Fear Is . . .

Spiders which crawl along the floor,
Also frogs drive me up the wall,
And dogs with feet that are worn and sore,
And slugs that slide under the door.
A millipede's legs
Which scare me half to death because
There are hundreds of them!
And boys with smelly breath.

Katie Rees (11)
Hartridge High School, Newport

Fear Is . . .

China dolls in shopping malls,
Like non-living women looking at me, so scary.
The Grim Reaper like a dead creature,
Sticky tape and getting raped.
The deadly syringe and the colour ginge!
This poem may be small,
But it has a meaning for us all!

Conor Thomas (11)
Hartridge High School, Newport

Fear Is . . .

Fear is huge spiders that creep and crawl,
Fear is scary ghosts lurking in the hall,
Fear is being locked in horrible cramped places,
Fear is meeting strange people, with horrid, unidentified faces,
Fear is false teeth that talk and chatter,
Fear is unknown noises that clutter and clatter.

Lois Ryan (12)
Hartridge High School, Newport

Fear Is . . .

Scary spiders that crawl up the wall,
Along with people about ten feet tall.
Smelly earwigs that crawl around in the winter,
Horrible, scary little splinters.

False teeth that fall out and bite,
Rats that bite all day and night.
Slimy slugs and snails that slime around in the rain,
Falling bricks which give me so much pain.

Red ants that bite people in the summer,
Playing computer games that make me even dumber.
Bullies that beat you up and give you a fright,
People who fly big, massive kites.

Very, very big heights,
Dead people who wake up in the night.
Men with big long nails,
Or animals with very long tails

Katie Boswell-Martin (11)
Hartridge High School, Newport

Fear Is . . .

Sharks that bite your legs off
Deadly smoke that makes you cough
China dolls sitting on the desk
Terrible tornados that destroy the rest.

Spiders that creep and crawl
Some people that beat you to the floor
Wolves that howl in the night
Vicious snakes that bite, bite, bite!

Clowns that jump in fun houses
Bungee-jumping, it always bounces
Thunderstorms that make you shake
Then there's the earthquake . . .

Liam Williams (12)
Hartridge High School, Newport

Dark Of Night

Fear today
Fear tonight
Fear of ghosts
No hall lights.

Beware of vampires, witches and the Devil
From evil coffins to broomsticks
And danger below ground level.

Fear! Fear! The spiders are here
From web to web
Closer and closer
Nearer and nearer.

Here's Chucky and his army of china dolls
This one's a killer
All you will see is his
Shadow in the mirror.

Finally the mice . . .
They will scratch and bite
Make sure you turn on the hall light!

Carla Woodruff (11)
Hartridge High School, Newport

Fear Is . . .

Spiders that are ugly and quite hairy,
Seagulls I think are scary,
Being stung by bees,
Eating nothing but cheese,
China dolls and a small clown,
People who smile and do not frown,
Being scared of wavy lines,
Poems that don't rhyme!

Leah Hutchinson (11)
Hartridge High School, Newport

Fear Is . . .

Spiders that are fat and hairy,
Let's get them, they are so scary.
Spinning webs in the corner of the room,
Let's get them with the vacuum.
But don't take too long, we don't want them to loom,
Or you could just get out of the room.

Pitch-black tunnels with freaky sounds,
They lead to freaky towns.
Can only go forward,
No going back,
Unless you want to run into pitch-black.

Being locked in a coffin,
And buried in the ground,
No one can hear you, not a sound.

Long words, especially smiles,
Because between s and s,
There is a mile!

Writing this poem in a straight way
Caused me much dismay!

Alexia Evans (12)
Hartridge High School, Newport

Fear Is . . .

Spiders because they are fat and hairy.
Ghosts because they are spooky and scary.
China dolls because they have eyes that are scary.
Slugs or snails because they are gooey and slimy.
Aeroplanes because they go high in the sky.
Rats and their tails.
I don't like the dark, so at night I use a torch-light.
I don't like long words, especially similes
Because in-between s and s there's a mile!

Lucy Henson (12)
Hartridge High School, Newport

Fear Is . . .

Slimy seaweed floating all around,
Ventriloquist dolls daring to make a sound,
Someone killing you in your sleep!

Getting lost and not being found,
Having solo phobia and being left alone
Feeling uncomfortable in your own home!

Being alone and hearing scary sounds,
Seeing death on your own doorstep,
With no one there to give you help!

Megan Kinsey (11)
Hartridge High School, Newport

Fear Is . . .

Country lanes, long and winding.
One-track roads, that can't be divided.

Potholing tunnels, all pitch-black.
Only one way forward . . .
No going back!

The pitch-black darkness, no light to be seen,
Can't see any objects, not something of which I'm keen.

Katie-Ann Blair (12)
Hartridge High School, Newport

Fear Is . . .

China dolls hanging on big, pale blue walls.
Green snakes slithering on a field floor.
Vampires' teeth chomping in the dark.
Small spaces, very scary.
Spiders crawling, creeping scary.
The Grim Reaper, very scary.
Wolves howling through the night.

Matthew Haynes (12)
Hartridge High School, Newport

Fear Is . . .

Fear is . . .
Fish that flip around,
Pigeons who make squawking sounds.
Snakes that slither around waiting for their prey
Spiders with their hairy legs.
Fear of drowning,
Fear of heights,
Fear of blood and guts,
And nasty mutts.
Squeaky mice that run about,
Fear of thunder and lightning at night,
Fear of clowns that go, *'Boo!'*
And a cockroach or two!

Emma Joy (12)
Hartridge High School, Newport

Fear Is . . .

Waking early in the morning
Earwigs creeping and evilly crawling
A big, dark place that is lonely
In the winter when it's cold
Cold feet shivering and bony
A huge black spider lurking, ready to kill
And a seagull with its evil shrill
Scared am I in school time
Sucking on a very sour lime
My sister looking like Frankenstein in the morning
And Ray Liotta in the film Unlawful Entry.

Elinor Spiers-Morgan (12)
Hartridge High School, Newport

Fear Is . . .

Clifftops high and full of rubble
When you look over, the height seems to double
Dry and dangerous, all cramped, not spacious.

Spiders scurrying fast and slow
With hairy legs and horrid faces
Loads are born every hour, they like to devour.

Great big animals everywhere
Bald on top, or with hair
Upturned eyes will make you sick
They pick at you as you wait for them to stop as the clock ticks.

Nadine Symonds (12)
Hartridge High School, Newport

Sweetie Peeps

The lollipop bounces around on one leg,
A big shiny nose, just like an egg.
Two small eyes with a great big smile,
That's my lollipop with candy cane arms.

The lollipop, he has a big round head,
He looks delicious as he lies in bed,
One little leg, great for a race,
Nothing can stop him from playing chase.

The place he lives is unknown to man,
He lives in the middle of a candy can,
A forest nearby,
Their jelly cars can fly,
Their place is called The Unknown Land.

Grace Brown (12)
Hreod Parkway School, Swindon

Inhabitants!

The tika is small and round,
It's only five inches off the ground.
It has no nose, and only three toes,
Short, sharp fur and googly eyes,
If he falls over, he's sure to cry.

His short little tail,
About the length of a nail.
He lives in a group,
And eats tomato soup.
That's the little tika,
Who lives on the island,
Of Costa Rica!

Karl Trevett (12)
Hreod Parkway School, Swindon

Soon, My Friend

As the moonlight hits the water
She waves her tail to say goodbye
And now you wish you'd never lied
For you and her come from different lands . . .
Yours one which she could never understand
You are not like her, she's not like you
And so you feel there is nothing you can do
Will you see her soon?
Who knows?
Who cares?
Well I do as I stare
Goodbye now, we'll meet again
I promise you, my new merfriend!

Hayley Bignell (12)
Hreod Parkway School, Swindon

Candy Cane Man

The Candy Cane Man is the one who knows,
Where everything is and where it goes,
Where he lives, no one knows,
On his six spiny toes.

His teeth are vile, orange and smelly,
Just like your dads very old welly,
His head is the size of a frying pan,
That's my creature, the Candy Cane Man.

Ciara Henderson (12)
Hreod Parkway School, Swindon

Rugby

We walk out standing proud,
We hear all the cheering from the crowd.

The match ball in the middle of the field,
The other team like a human shield.

It started; I was in a massive fright,
They came running at me looking for a fight!

Declan Turner (13)
Ibstock Community College, Ibstock

Swimming!

Splish, splash, splosh
Diving through the pool
Swimming past the post
Being a dolphin doing a back flip
Swimming is so much fun
My goggles have come undone.

Rebecca Sales (11)
Ibstock Community College, Ibstock

Poetry

P is for poetry, for laughter and fun.
O is for onomatopoeia.
E is for extraordinary entertainment.
T is for talent so brilliant.
R is for rhyme and rhythm.
Y is for yawning, sleeping and snoring.

I is for ideas and inspiration.
S is for speaking, laughing and chatting.

C is for communication.
O is for ogre, creeps and slime.
O is for original, shiny and new.
L is for lazy days with a sea view.

Amy Whitehouse (11)
Ibstock Community College, Ibstock

My Dog Midnight

M idnight is the dippiest dog you will ever find.
I nstead of thinking about things, Midnight goes straight into things
headfirst, literally!
D ippy is the word to explain my dog Midnight.
N aughty all over, especially when she chews your shoes.
I think that Midnight's the best dog you will ever find.
G orgeous is what Midnight is because of her blue eyes and
the colour of her fur.
H ow lazy do dogs get? Because you won't find a dog lazier
than Midnight.
T otally cuddly and cute plus dippy is everything that explains
Midnight, my dog!

Emma Cox (13)
Ibstock Community College, Ibstock

The Sea

The sea has a split personality,
One is calming and relaxing,
The other rough and frightening,
Sending a chill down your spine.

The sea is like a zoo
With exotic animals,
The plants eventually
Float to the top almost saying,
'Look at me, I'm here!'

The sea is like a mirror,
It copies the colour of the sky,
Not showing its true colours.

The sea is like a blanket,
Smothering drowning people,
Carrying everything with it.

Magical myths whisper along the ocean,
Of creatures like mermaids,
The women with a tail,
Kings of the ocean like
Neptune and Poseidon.

Sarah Gray (13)
Ibstock Community College, Ibstock

Untitled

M ardy people
O h no
N asty lads
D umb revision
A aah, help
Y esterday's news
S illy teachers.

Georgie Rowley (11)
Ibstock Community College, Ibstock

My World

You wanna step into my world
It's a psychotic frenzy
You've been time-tracked in the real world
You ain't seen what happens to me.

The coldness of my loneliness
Scares me half to death
I don't have no holiness
Cos the Devil's under my breath.

If you're gonna enter my world
You might turn yourself insane
Cos there ain't no peace in my world
Just a hole inside your brain.

I bet you think I'm telling lies
That it's all inside my head
Well it's taken me time to realise
That really I am dead!

Zoe Cooper (13)
Ibstock Community College, Ibstock

What Could It Be?

The girl stood alone
In the bitter wind
She heard a noise
Like the scattering of bones
A wolf crept up on her
But it did no harm
She heard another noise
But nothing was in sight
What could it be?

Lucy Girvan (12)
Ibstock Community College, Ibstock

A Day Fishing

Find the spot that's got the lot
A river and some shade
I'm going to catch a big one now
I think I've got it made.
Settle my chair
Straighten my flask
Pray for the sunshine
That's all I can ask.
The big one's there
Just for the getting
By the end of the day
It'll be in my netting.

It's turning cold and very grey
The weather's going to spoil my day.
Well anyway, the fish can be glad
He's the biggest trophy I never had!

Dale Hudson (13)
Ibstock Community College, Ibstock

Poverty

On this day
Words were spoken
Music was played.
In nine different places
People came to help.
They all wanted to be there
Through thick and thin
To help the poor
With trouble and aid.
The trouble has gone on too long
Make poverty history
Sooner, not later.

Nicole Tubby (12)
Ibstock Community College, Ibstock

In Lands Of Old

Once upon a time,
In lands of old,
There lived a knight,
Strong and bold.

He came across,
A shady bower,
And deep inside,
A stately tower.

The door he opened,
Climbed the stairs,
Joined a lady,
With golden hair.

With bright blue eyes,
Young and fair,
With ribbons twined,
Between her hair.

His chest stuck out,
Took her arm,
Whispered softly,
'Please stay calm.'

They rode off,
But do not fret,
They will be back,
Just not yet . . .

Zoë Ross-Finucane (12)
Ibstock Community College, Ibstock

Hobbies - Haiku

Tennis, PlayStation
Are my favourite hobbies
Grand Theft Auto - brill!

Daniel O'Hara (12)
Ibstock Community College, Ibstock

My Mum's Not Here Today

My mum's not here today,
Well, not here anymore,
You see a bad thing happened to her,
Yeah, she died in the war!

This might have happened to your mum or dad,
It's not fair I know!
But why, oh why my mum?
I really loved her so!

My dad is really upset,
He cries every day!
I really want to help him,
But I don't know what to say.

I really loved my mum,
She was very close to me,
When my mother was here,
We were as happy as can be!

Jessica Woolerton (11)
Ibstock Community College, Ibstock

Leicester Are The Best!

Leicester are the best,
Whenever they're against Derby,
Derby play like Barbie,
Man U are the worst,
And Leicester are first,
Danny Tiatto is cool,
But Ian Walker is a fool,
Rooney is ok
But Giggs is gay,
Leicester are the best,
And can beat all the rest!

Thomas Hunt (12)
Ibstock Community College, Ibstock

Never Have I Fallen

Your lips speak soft sweetness
Your touch a cool caress
I am lost in your magic
My heart beats within your chest.

I think of you each morning
And dream of you each night
I think of your arms being around me
And cannot express my delight.

Never have I fallen
But I am quickly on my way
You hold a heart in your hands
That has never before been given away.

Daniel Clemow (13)
Ibstock Community College, Ibstock

Make Poverty History

We are all kind inside
So give a little helping hand
To the people in Africa.

They have no food or water
They will go to sleep tonight starving
And then the next night and then the next
For the rest of their short lives.
So just think that every three seconds
One person dies in Africa
Most of them are children,
So, make poverty history and say *no!*

Jessica Bradford (12)
Ibstock Community College, Ibstock

Pollution

The world is coming to an end,
The damage we cannot mend,
Pollution fills the vital air,
Oh why does no one seem to care?
Animals and people die every day,
From pollution coming in from the bay
People try to find another way,
But no one hears what they say.
How could this happen, how?
We need to stop this *now!*
Save the world is what we should aim for,
But the pollution gets more and more
Mother Nature is very sad,
As lots of people are very bad,
The world will come to an end,
Unless pollution stops *now!*

Max Nissen (12)
Ibstock Community College, Ibstock

A Snowman

There's a snowman in my garden
He's moving side to side
I don't know what he's doing
But I think he's trying to hide!

Maybe he's just scared of me
Or maybe he's just sad
Maybe the sun is melting him
But I think he's rather mad!

Katie Smith (12)
Ibstock Community College, Ibstock

Bends

I was jealous of my little brother,
Better at everything than me,
He got a job on a boat,
Diving into the sea.

Mum and Dad were proud of him,
I was silently pleased,
We went and watched him from the shore,
When he got taken away by the sea.

I screamed and screamed but nothing came out,
I knew that something was wrong,
People came out on lifeboats,
It seemed to take so long.

He tried to come up but his foot was stuck,
And when he got out he had the bends,
We sat in the room whilst he slept,
When the machine bleeped, 'twas the end.

Rosie Buck (12)
Ibstock Community College, Ibstock

How Summer Died

The leaves began to turn brown,
And the temperature started to cool down.
There was a chill in the air,
And the birds were aware.

The plants started to die,
And the birds sung, 'Bye, bye!'
The fruit became ripe,
And varied in type.

Water started to fall from the sky
And I just thought, *why?*

Luke Dodd (12)
Ibstock Community College, Ibstock

Fish In The Sea

Fish, fish swimming in the sea,
Colours like a rainbow
Shining like a Christmas tree
In the deep blue sea
Colours like a rainbow
Shining like a Christmas tree
In the deep blue sea
Gushing
Their tails splish-splash - splashing in the deep blue sea.

Mark Shaw (12)
Ibstock Community College, Ibstock

Death

Her eyes closed,
Her hand lost grip,
Her smile weakened,
Her heart lost beats,
Her face was pale,
As she drifted off to sleep,
Never to wake up,
The flowers around her shrivelled and died,
As she did when she left our side.

Racheal Morris (12)
Ibstock Community College, Ibstock

Shark

S wimming sea predators
H unting for food
A ggressive
R ipping sharp teeth
K illing, giant jaws.

Scott Findley (12)
Ibstock Community College, Ibstock

Nibbles

Nibbles is a Russian dwarf
He's very, very tiny.
He's got red eyes
And he's grey and white.
His teeth are sharp and shiny.
Nibbles, Nibbles on your fingers
And often on your toes.
He scrambles up your trouser leg
And off into your pocket and in he goes,
There, he drops off to sleep.
Till that hand decides to land
In the pocket and out again,
And in the cage he lands!

Fraser Shaw (12)
Ibstock Community College, Ibstock

My First And Last Love

The day started off
As a normal day
The alarm clock woke me up
As the sun shone through my bedroom window
But what I did not know was
That today I would meet him
Who? You may ask
David, of course
Shall I kiss him?
I thought or should I ask him round for tea
What should I do?

Laura Ball (12)
Ibstock Community College, Ibstock

Night

Wind howls and lightning squeals
Rain pours down and evil prevails
Drown the cockerel, on the spire
Nights like these
I never remember having seen.

Little Susie says goodbye
Golden curls gone red
Falls down the stairs
Head hits the floor
'Susie,' she cried
But only I heard
Someone killed little Susie that night
Nights like these
I never remember having seen.

Abigail Allen (12)
Ibstock Community College, Ibstock

Quads

Quads go fast
Cars start to crash
They bomb along
While you sing a song
Bugs go in your face
You feel a big disgrace
Your tyres burst
You start to curse
You're face to face against an opponent
This is your special moment!

Mathew Pioli (12)
Ibstock Community College, Ibstock

The Sad Tale

One snowy night
In the freezing cold
A boy lay on the pavement
Shivering with fear
Dying slowly from starvation.

Every car that comes by
Stares at him and tooted
No one ever threw a coin to him
Not even a penny.

I felt sorry for him
So I said to myself
Tomorrow I would give him food.

Tomorrow came
I went to him
But I was too late
He was dead . . .

Lindsey Else (12)
Ibstock Community College, Ibstock

Cancer

Taking over your body like water rising,
Not stopping until it's got you whole,
Eating you up all inside you,
Not leaving any left to keep your soul,
What's it done to you, what's it done?
Taken your family and your fun,
Why, oh why did it happen to me?
Life's as unfair as it can be!

Lorna Wiltshire (12)
Ibstock Community College, Ibstock

Boys

Boys are in a totally different world,
They like to play football,
Don't like netball,
Always get mauled.

Boys get fought over,
They like to be alone,
Always have a lover,
Never answer the phone.

Don't listen to their mother,
Always out,
Annoying their brothers,
Like to shout,
Never do any other!

What's the point?
They don't like any fame.
They'll never read this anyway!

Linnette Sleigh (12)
Ibstock Community College, Ibstock

Australia

A ustralia
U nited with England
S urfing the waves
T rees full of koala bears
R eefs full of colourful fish
A rainbow island
L eaping kangaroos
I ncredible, clear-blue seas
A mazing animals everywhere.

Lorna Jones (12)
Ibstock Community College, Ibstock

My Dog Maizie

M y dog Maizie is very active
Y oung and loves football but . . .

D oes not like swimming
O ver the fields she runs
G rabbing a stick as she goes.

M y dog Maizie
A nd the others
I n the house
Z zzz is the noise they make
I n their baskets
E very night asleep.

Heather Fox (12)
Ibstock Community College, Ibstock

The Park

Hanging in the park,
Swing, swing
Whoosh, whoosh.
Hanging in the park
Mates all around
What to do?
What to do?
Hanging in the park
Finding the spot
Finding the spot.
Hanging in the park,
Don't forget to have fun!

Ellis Roulston (13)
Ibstock Community College, Ibstock

Fox!

Closer, closer, fox is creeping,
To the baby rabbit, sleeping.

The rabbit dreams without a care,
Despite the fox's deadly glare.

To get this very tasty meal,
The rabbit's life he'll have to steal.

Suddenly rabbit's wide awake,
Now the fox's meal's at stake.

Quickly, fox tries to bound,
To pin the rabbit to the ground.

But rabbit's gone in a flash,
To get his dinner, fox must dash.

Rabbit races to the hole
And burrows down it like a mole.

Fox can only slope away,
He'll go hungry for another day.

Katie Dennis (11)
Leicester High School for Girls, Leicester

Orphan Child

Orphan child, sitting on his bed
No one to love, everyone to hate
Family all dead
Windows dusty, no light shines on his head
His heart has grown cold
Orphan child, sitting on his bed.

Orphan teenager, sitting on his bed
No friends to talk to
Family still dead
He sits on his bed with himself for company
His heart is nearly frozen
Orphan teenager, sitting on his bed.

Orphan adult, sitting on his bed
No family of his own
Family still dead
Sitting on his bed, like it's all he has left
His heart about to smash
Orphan adult, sitting on his bed.

Poor little orphan lying in his grave,
No one came to his funeral
No one said goodbye
Lying in his grave, dead at last
His heart has melted
Poor little orphan, lying in his grave.

Tessa Hawkes (11)
Leicester High School for Girls, Leicester

Rainbow

Red flowers, how they grow in spring,
Like tulips and roses arriving.

Orange is the colour of a fruit,
With the smell of my dad's new suit.

The sun is the colour yellow,
Like the voice of a young fellow.

Green is like the grass all growing,
Trees and plants are now showing.

The wind is blowing which is blue,
It's just like the colour of my old shoe.

Indigo sounds like a thunderstorm,
Making a sound like a horn.

Vile violet devouring its way,
Pushing us out and making us sway.

Bhakti Daudia (12)
Leicester High School for Girls, Leicester

Chocolate

The creamy sensation
It is such a temptation
White, brown, dark
It always seems better than just plain bark!
You'll never get sick of it
Don't just take a little bit
With the taste the size of a football pitch
It makes you feel so rich

It *looks* like chocolate
It *feels* like chocolate
It *smells* like chocolate
It *tastes* like chocolate

It is chocolate!

Sarina Dayah (11)
Leicester High School for Girls, Leicester

The Circle Of Life

In a world full of sin right from the start,
Did we ever have hope with no peace in our hearts?
People are divided by religion and faith,
They pray to their gods but receive no answer.
People are punished for their harmless banter,
How long must we live to see a perfect world?
For a horse to be whipped but for it not to canter,
In a world full of war causing pain every day,
But for suits and ties to still receive their pay.
The black oblivion versus the grey apocalypse,
The ageing rule book now shredded to bits,
As the disciples and followers turn to crime,
No longer religious, they are oblivious to time,
But crying out wherever they go,
'Only God can judge, I have no foe.'
How easy can Hell be if this is our world?
How hard can Heaven be if this is our world?
Years go by and they're wasted,
And people start to realise,
It's their lives which have been created;
But now it's too late,
Their time has been and gone,
They could've made a change,
But in this world they no longer belong.

Hannah Culley (12)
Leicester High School for Girls, Leicester

The Rainbow

Red is the colour of love,
Nice and peaceful as a dove.

Orange is the colour of a tiger,
Dangerous as a fire.

Yellow is the colour of sunrays,
When children go out to play.

Green is the colour of grass,
The children pick it as they pass.

Blue is the colour of the sea,
People sit there as they have their tea.

Indigo is the colour of a flower,
You can see them if you stand high on a tower.

Violet is the colour of the sky,
You can see it if you fly high.

Sonal Shah (11)
Leicester High School for Girls, Leicester

Without You . . .

(Inspired by 'Stop All The Clocks' by W H Auden)

The sky is no longer an azure blue
And the sun does not shine with its golden hue
The stars in the night sky shine no more
And gone is the wind that we both adored . . .

The flowers have ceased to bloom in a vibrant array
And the poets are left with nothing to say
The mountains no more meet the blue sky
And the birds have forgotten to sing and fly . . .

The rain no more brings a touch of romance, the moon has lost its shine
And each day my hope to meet you is dying
The world's beauty has faded since the distance between us grew
And my life seems incomplete just because there is no you.

Tehseena Mulla (15)
Moat Community College, Leicester

Stuck Between Two Worlds

(Inspired by 'Two Worlds' by Shahana Mirza)

I am stuck between two worlds
Caught up between two lives
Like a lift stuck high up a building
I don't dare to look down
Coz I'm scared, man
Seems like my life is hanging in the balance
But I seem to always look up to my family and religion
Which way do I go, up or down?

But sometimes I am forced to look down
But pull back, as I am scared to drown in this unknown western world
This western world I know nothing of
We've lost our mouth and face
We've lost our culture but not our race
It is like a complicated maze
I did contribute but still don't feel part of it!

I'm struggling to find my way through it
Trying to find my way out
Left or right, which way will lead me to my chosen life?
I will have to make that unwanted dive down below
Will it kill my culture and language?
Keep on going my own way but lose something to get there
Or do I climb up to safety?
I still haven't decided and it's stressing me out, dude!

Mohamed Samatar (15)
Moat Community College, Leicester

Lonely

(Inspired by 'Two Worlds' by Shahana Mirza)

I have two worlds
In my mind
I feel so different
Alone inside.
Why these feelings? I need to know
Now I'll see what I don't know.

It seems I have two everything
Two languages
And two of simple things.
I have two names
I have two ways of dressing
But what is there that I have that's the same?

My family is around all the time
They are so different to me inside
I just want to get away
To a world not so far away.

Alone inside? I'm not so sure.
Am I divided? I feel so sore.
It seems out there I'm not alone.
Others alike but I don't know?
Maybe one day I'll find out
Who is me?

Tahmina Begum-Ali (15)
Moat Community College, Leicester

A Child's Wish

'If I were Superman, Mama,
I'd fly us away
I'd take us to a better place
Where starvation is at bay.
If I were a millionaire, Mama,
I'd buy us the sun
I'd bring the light into everyone's lives
So we are equal, all one.'

'If I were king, Mama,
I'd take care of my people
I'd ensure their wealth and health
And rule a place where there were no unhappy people.
If I were a star, Mama,
I'd brighten everyone's life
I'd ensure all happiness
And make sure sadness was out of sight.'

'I wish that to conquer life wasn't an obstacle, Mama,
To live one day wasn't cruel
To strive to feed our mouths wasn't hard
To taste a drop was a rule.
Why do you cry, Mama? Why are there tears in your eyes?
All I want is to take us to a safer place
Where there is no pain, hunger and crime
I wish it with my heart, Mama
I wish it to be true!'

'Do you have a wish, Mama? Do you have a dream too?
Do you hope for a miracle to happen, Mama?
And wish the world were a secure place
Where evil did not exist and for good to happen was not just a wish?'

My mama smiled at me and said,
'There is no greater wish that a mother could wish for,
Than to have you.'

Shanaz Rahman (15)
Moat Community College, Leicester

Their Battles Are Ongoing

(Inspired by 'Two Worlds' by Shahana Mirza)

You've got the best of both worlds
I tell myself
But the weight of these two worlds
Can be too heavy to bear
You all know me as Durgha
But the real me is Durgha

My feelings are not balanced
Nor are my actions
Pulled in two different directions
Finding it hard to choose
When the scales tip to one side
I'm not doing justice to the other

In the same moment
Reaching success and failure
Gaining love and hate
Living here in the cold
But longing to be there in the warmth
Loving it here with my friends
But desperately wishing for my missed experiences there

Will this raging storm ever pass?
Will my dreams ever come true?
Will I see everything I want to see?
Or will my two worlds imprison me?

My two worlds fuse, clash or separate
Their battles are ongoing
But what my future holds for me
Only time can tell.

Durgha Ramji (15)
Moat Community College, Leicester

Broken, Bruised And Shattered . . .

Sometimes when I close my eyes,
I feel myself rise.
I pray you were around,
So I could cherish the sound
Of your voice.
I wish it was my choice!

Everybody says 'give it some time'.
I am fed up with hearing this chime.
Do they not know,
How hard it is to let go and bow
To the hard fact that you left?
It is indeed a theft,
As you stole my heart.

My emotions are sometimes too much to bear!
I thought this love was so rare.
Alas, I was wrong!
Understanding you took me so long.
Precious is what you are to me,
Your face is what I long to see.
With this feeling inside,
I feel you alongside.

Everyone can see through my eyes,
The sadness that lies.
Still they question me so many times,
'Why have you been left aside by the tides?'
This question leaves me with nothing to say.
'Let no one ask me about this ever again,' to God I pray.
I am never going to fall in love again,
Never going to be wrong again.
I'll never feel this pain,
As my heart is like a broken windowpane.
Broken, bruised and shattered . . .

Tasneem Woozeer (15)
Moat Community College, Leicester

Terrorism

Terrorism scares us all.
We are not afraid,
Though we know there's much to fear.
As I look out the window,
And see how much this world has developed,
I wonder, will it stay like this?
I can see ruins of houses,
Grey skies, people crying and ambulances rushing.

When I go out for a walk or on a bus,
Train or plane I think,
Will I get home safely?
Or will I be another number on a list?
Will people mourn over me?
Or will I be the one mourning?
There's nothing we can do but pray and hope.

Going to school, college, work, anywhere,
We should stand tall,
And show them we can go through it all,
Like the strong people we are.

Sara Saleh (14)
Newborough School, Woolton

The London Bombings

Second after second passes slowly by,
The bus blows up on the 7th July.
Death's victims rising quick,
The bomb goes off with a click.
Tears drop as people die,
Like World War II the shrapnel flies.
Terrorism is what people say,
Minutes ago, children played.
On the streets everything's bad,
Drenched with blood: wallets, coats and a handbag.
Lights are flashing at passers-by,
The clouds take over the sky.
This is the night that killed someone's wife,
This is the night that ruined someone's life.

Fabian Sabbara (12)
Rutlish School, Merton Park

The Summer Of Friendship

We can go . . .
Shopping in Paris
Or cruising the Med.
Or skiing in Finland
Or snowboardin' instead.
Just as long as I'm with
A couple of friends,
We'll have an awesome summer
Till the end!

We can go . . .
Surfing in Sydney
Or just catch some rays
Or partying in Ibiza
Or drink coffee all day.
Just as long as I'm with
A couple of friends,
We'll have a rockin' summer
Till the end!

We can go . . .
Swimming with dolphins
Or diving with sharks
Or chilling on beaches
Or skating in parks.
Just as long as I'm with
A couple of friends,
We'll have the greatest summer
Till the end!

Kim Akwei-Howe (14)
St Benet Bishop Catholic High School, Bedlington

Summer Sonnet

Summer holidays are extremely fun,
For seven whole weeks there's no boring school,
Shouting and laughing, great fun in the sun,
Splashing and playing in the swimming pool.
No more dull black clouds, just clear, sunny skies,
Eating ice cream on the hot, golden sands,
Over seven seas, the aeroplane flies,
In sunny hot Spain the aeroplane lands.
I put on some suncream so I don't burn,
I take off my cap, it's just far too hot,
On the cool rides I feel my stomach turn,
It's really hard to find a shaded spot.
The steaming hot sun starts to burn my neck,
My shoulders go red-hot, oh bloomin' heck!

Michael Gandy (12)
St Ninian's High School, Giffnock

Summer Sonnet

As midsummer draws nearer and nearer,
And the nights grow short as the days grow long,
And the bright skies grow clearer and clearer,
No need to answer questions right or wrong,
Relaxing long in the burning hot sun,
Fervently wishing summer never stops,
Going to theme parks and having much fun,
And eating lots of large, sweet lollipops,
Buying candyfloss, enjoying myself,
Now as my holiday comes to its end,
Finding souvenirs to put on my shelf,
Wasting the money I have left to spend,
Finally, I pack my bags, leave for home,
Longing for the bedroom I call my own.

Alan McCabe (12)
St Ninian's High School, Giffnock

Summer Sonnet

The bright, yellow sun blinds me in the sky
The deep blue sea twinkles under its rays
Flying up in the air, the plane so high
Sunbathing on the beach for days and days
Relaxing by the pool for days on end
Building sandcastles on the beach, much fun
Ice cream dripping, you forget to attend
Have to go and swim, the heat of the sun
Eating out at posh restaurants late night
Burning your feet on the boiling hot sand
Can't go without sunglasses, it's so bright
You go to bed, don't want it to end and
Before you know it, you're back on the plane
You are back in Scotland, back in the rain.

Suzanne Oswald (12)
St Ninian's High School, Giffnock

Summer Sonnet

One day left, I am nearly back at home . . .
In a hot classroom thinking days to come -
Of sunny seaside waves tipped with white foam,
Cold ice creams and big days out, lots of fun.
To France I go, to see all the big sights,
Eiffel Tower, Le Louvre, cannot wait,
Going for tea every beautiful night,
Holiday is going to be just great.
At the beach, along with bucket and spade,
Then writing my postcards with all I've done -
The sun is so hot, I stay in the shade,
Resting after my long day in the sun.
I think France is so very, very hot,
Coming back now with the gifts I have bought!

Marie-Claire Flynn (13)
St Ninian's High School, Giffnock

Summer Sonnet

Going away to somewhere far away,
Barcelona, Ireland, Millport, there too.
I'm going on my summer holiday,
Clothes, hats, shoes, sunglasses, they're all brand new.
Seeing Great Britain as a tiny dot,
Going on holiday, really can't wait.
Going to the beach when it's really hot,
Eating ice cream and talking to my mate.
Sun going down at eleven o'clock,
Visiting all the sights in the city.
Going around town, though I have to walk,
I am going home soon, what a pity.
So before school we can have some more fun,
You know the holidays are number one!

Kaitlyn Dynes (13)
St Ninian's High School, Giffnock

Summer Sonnet

Under a tree, staying in the cool shade,
Wearing a hat to protect from the sun,
Making sandcastles with bucket and spade,
Having a BBQ is so much fun!
Munching on a punnet of strawberries,
Slurping on a pineapple ice cream - yum!
Sitting, absently swatting wasps and bees,
'Get out of the sun now!' hollers my mum.
I cannot wait to escape back to Spain,
A whole sweltering day spent sightseeing,
Unfortunate - flight's at seven again!
Then the rest of the break spent sunbathing.
Having races with brother in the pool,
After a hot day, it is very cool!

Laura Martin (12)
St Ninian's High School, Giffnock

Summer Sonnet

Summer is super - the time to relax
The weather is wonderful, it's such fun
Drinking fresh fruit juice and munching on snacks
Getting a tan in the warm summer sun.
Slapping on plenty of suntanning cream
I lie in a hammock in the garden
This day is really a wonderful dream
I eat my ice cream and can't help but grin.
How I would love to dive into a pool
Just longing for that wonderful cold splash
I am so hot, I just want to be cool
Buckets and spades have used up all my cash.
I love the summer, the best of seasons
Could say why but there's too many reasons!

Ruth Leiser (13)
St Ninian's High School, Giffnock

Archaon, Lord Of The End Times

Archaon attacked the castle, hard and quick
His huge army amassed on the field
With their swords, spears, shields, catapults and other equipment
The Prince of Darkness swept in from the north, destroying all
in his path
His dark gods, Khorne, Tzeencth, Slaneesh and Nurgle, united
behind him
And would make him a god if he succeeded and destroyed the
city of Midgar.

He slayed the servants of his enemies easily
His huge sword shook ominously with power
The demon inside longed to be released from its prison.

The Prince of Hell had not been found in city, castle, palace or port
He was found in a cave, crawling around as a baby
His finder, Malek, and his malicious war band said he had no
family, nothing
But he was destined to dominate and conquer
He would herald the apocalypse and take over.

Boulders battered against the walls and bows beleaguered the city
Demons demanded to slaughter whatever they could
Drums were drummed, horns were sounded, the armies'
morale heightened.

Shaun Clerkin (13)
St Ninian's High School, Kirkintilloch

Rikumaru

He was trying to find the key to Hinuka's lair
He was trying to get to the princess' prison
If he didn't, the world couldn't win
It will never prevail if the princess is kept
Rikumaru was the best, but surely he could not do it
Saviour with the samurai, the only one that could
He was crawling along houses, swinging from roof to roof
King of kung fu was winning just for now
But the evil Knievel had a plan to kill
King of samurai had found the key
The ninja was getting closer to his needed goal
But then Hinuka sprang his surprise
Archers all around him
Rikumaru gave them his gift
A sticky bomb for brutes
Now it was no problem
Only Hinuka could halt him now
And he was no ninja
So he picked up the princess and took her home
Now the world is winning and forever will.

Brian McFadden (12)
St Ninian's High School, Kirkintilloch

Bits Of Early Days

(Inspired by 'Bits of Early Days' by James Berry)

Still a shock to remember, being
Told I didn't have a
Grandad anymore;
Being told I'm gonna
Be an auntie for the first time

Still a joy to remember holding
My second nephew;
And following my sister
Down the aisle on her
Wedding day.

Still a shock to remember, the first
Solid food tickling
My throat.
Walking into my first
Day at primary school.

Still a joy to remember, dancing
To Happy Birthday in
Spain.
Taking baby steps
And laughing at
The patterned ducks diving.

Still a pain to have,
A pain in my stomach
Being poked by sterile doctors
And stared at by shiny machines;
I wish to forget.

Laura Kelly (13)
Sheldon School, Chippenham

Memories

Still a shock to remember,
The squirrel clambering
Over the branches,
And the moment when
It dropped a conker
On my head.

Still a joy to remember
The large brown eyes
Of our old dog
Coming home.

Still a shock to remember
The metal gleam
On our fence
As it charged at 360v!

Still a joy to remember
The jump, plummet,
The flash of green
And the blurred springback,
On the bungee jump.

Still weird to remember
The moment the llama dropped
Onto my shoulder
And hopped off.

Matthew Pickering (12)
Sheldon School, Chippenham

A Poem Called 'The Cellar'

A stormy night, when thunder roars,
A lonely house, sits upon the moors,
The candles flicker, the floorboards creak,
The spirit, a victim, starts to seek.

A lady sits by a dimming fire,
Her eyelids flicker, she starts to tire.
Is that the wind or a baby's cry,
The pelting rain or a woman's sigh?

The lady stands, transfixed with fear,
A wispy vision has appeared.
The lady knows she has to follow,
The ghostly vision, with cheeks so hollow.

Down to the cellar, the spirit glides,
The lady follows, with eyes wide open.
The spirit stops and looks around,
And points a finger to the ground.

All went dark, the spirit's gone,
The lady knew her job was done.
She marked the spot, so in the day,
She'd know, beneath the ground, what lay!

Removed to the church where she is blessed,
The spirit now, at last can rest.

Catherine Carey (13)
Sheldon School, Chippenham

Memories

I can still remember the horror of being chased by a bull in a field -
The lump of hoof, tusk, bone and muscle
Pounding the muddy ground,
Earth flying through the air.

I can still remember the joy of seeing my dad's friend's Dalmatians
Bounding towards me -
The crunch of gravel, the wagging tails, the soft feeling of fur,
The panting and the wet, slimy tongues.

I can still remember the strange feeling of cutting my chin
After going head-over-heels on my trike,
The blood, the pain, lying on the pavement
And the doctor gluing my chin together.

I can still remember the anger every time I see a cat
Using the garden as its toilet
And then you step in it -
The smell, the *shlurp* sound, the hours it takes to clean
And the cat's evil, slit eyes.

Rhys Merriman (12)
Sheldon School, Chippenham

My Life

Still a shock to remember my dad walking out with nothing
But the clothes he was wearing.
Still a surprise to remember my mum screeching
With no reason for it.
Still a shock to remember seeing a blurry world
As I was dragged to the surface.
Still a surprise to remember dreaming of drifting through the clouds
And the air in my power.
Still a shock to remember my brother only just waking up
After being put to sleep, the horrid cuts above his eyes.
Still a surprise to remember everybody rushing after one man
And me not knowing what happened.

Lisa King (12)
Sheldon School, Chippenham

Memories

I can still remember the joy
Of her gummy mouth opening,
Smiling at me, wide and toothless.

I can still remember the shock
Of tripping on a rock and smashing my head on a brick,
Blood gushing down my shirt.

I can still remember the joy
Of gracefully riding it, my shiny new BMX,
Zooming down the road.

I can still remember the shock
Of the feathered creature advancing towards me,
Crying and pecking at my legs.

I can still remember the joy
Of stepping out of the village church on Christmas Day,
Snowflakes glistening down.

I can still remember the shock
Of the poor victim of the hawk,
Being ripped apart, guts flying.

I can still remember the joy
Of being told my treat,
Euro Disney for Christmas pleased my mind.

I can still remember the shock
Of the ball speeding towards my wrist,
The simple but painful snap.

I can still remember the joy
Of nursing a broken wing,
Charlie finch recovering with my help.

I can still remember the shock
Of losing Mum's hand, people all around,
Standing alone in the large supermarket.

Tiffany Burrows (12)
Sheldon School, Chippenham

I Can Still Remember

I can still remember feeling joy when I got my dog,
The soft, black puppy jumping up at you,
The food on her nose and her sad little eyes.

I can still remember feeling sad when my hamsters died,
Their stiff bodies curled up in my hand,
Their fur cold and their feet curled up.

I can still remember feeling joy when I swam with dolphins,
Holding their fins and getting pulled along,
Watching them jump and catch the fish after doing tricks.

I can still remember feeling sad when my friend moved away,
No best friend to talk to, always second best,
Losing touch and not seeing each other again.

I can still remember feeling fear when I went on a roller coaster,
The long climb up waiting for the drop,
Falling, falling, falling and wanting to go again!

I can still remember feeling shock when I hurt myself,
One minute playing, the next I'd whacked my face
On the corner of the table,
The pain and shock just struck me.

I can still remember feeling fear when I thought someone
Broke into my house,
The creak of the stairs, the murmur of voices,
Me and my sister at home alone.

I can still remember feeling shock when England won
The World Cup,
The one try, the penalties, the drop goals,
The shock and happiness.

Emma Boyd (12)
Sheldon School, Chippenham

I Can Still Remember

I can still remember the surprise
Of my birthday presents, the speedy
Blue wheels of my Rollerblades.

I can still remember the happiness
Of going to Disneyland with my
Friends and family.

I can still remember the warm glow
I felt inside when I held baby
Carys as she slept peacefully in my arms.

I can still remember the sadness
When Lucky, my white-striped hamster,
Died in summer 2003.

I can still remember the shock
When we saw a dead grey tabby cat
Staring unseeingly.

I can still remember the joy
Of my cousin's new life
Glowing with love.

Eve Griffith (12)
Sheldon School, Chippenham

The Seagull

Creeping about in the dead of night,
Creeping about to give you a fright,
Searching around for an eye that fits,
He's coming for you, he'll rip you to bits!
How do you know, he might be round the corner,
Doesn't matter who you are, Tom, Bob or Lorna,
He's going to get you, he's coming for you,
Watch out for telltale droplets of poo!

Roxanne Barrett & Rachel Plowright (12)
Sheldon School, Chippenham

The Wind's Bad Mood

The wild horse
Galloped over the plain
The wind racing it desperately
And losing
Hid and sulked
In the leaves.

The pink pig
Rootled inside the yard
The wind throwing the turnips
And howling
Hid and sulked
In the trough.

The black cat
Slept serenely by the fire
The wind rattling the windows
And groaning
Hid and sulked
In the bin.

The little puppy
Frolicked in the garden
The wind blowing the yellow ball
And panting
Hid and sulked
In the daisies.

The tiny hamster
Squeaked in the cage
The wind spinning the wheel
And sighing
Hid and sulked
In the bowl.

Ruth Emerson (12)
Sheldon School, Chippenham

I Can Vaguely Remember

I can still remember the joy in my heart
When I stepped out of the aeroplane,
The moist, brown soil and the sturdy palm trees were mine,
India, my motherland.

I can still remember the beggarman's eyes,
Filled with eternal tears,
Whilst we struggled to swallow,
The guilt in the air was painful,
He was lucky to have a morsel.

I can still remember the feeling of perseverance and integrity,
It had all paid off,
And my heart was beating so fast,
My black belt was inches away.

I can still remember the sweet smell of roses,
Holland, the beautiful country,
Glowing with passion and colour,
How I miss these fantastic moments!

Vasantha Lanka (12)
Sheldon School, Chippenham

Memories

I can still remember the long grass tickling my tanned cheeks
On a warm summer's day.
I can still remember the shock of seeing a dead baby sparrow
Being slowly devoured by a cat; it froze me to the spot.
I can still remember the beauty of the sea from the hilltop, glittering,
Shimmering like a huge mirror magnified ten thousand times.
I can still remember the horror of passing a dead cat,
Its eyes staring deep into the mists of unseeing life.
I can still remember the joy of winning pass-the-parcel
When I was three,
The soft fur of the cuddly toy I had won.

Ruth Knight (12)
Sheldon School, Chippenham

Hooves In The Seasons

Hooves are glistening,
In the winter months,
Shiny in the ice,
And soft in the snow.

Hooves are getting hard to find,
Among the springtime joy,
In amongst the pretty flowers,
And nearby every little foot.

Hooves are all so clear now,
Upon the crispy grass,
All so bright and green,
As long as the summer lasts.

Hooves are all hidden now,
Beneath the autumn leaves,
Covered in leaves so bright,
On top of all the mud.

Leanne Scoynes (12)
Sheldon School, Chippenham

Sunny Sunflowers

(Inspired by the painting 'Sunflowers' by Van Gogh)

Golden-yellow petals,
Golden, glowing balls of flame.
Orange, rusty centres,
Like dying hearts, like faces.

Fiery, bright, burning sunflowers,
Dressed all in gold.
Petals like knotted hair,
Sharp as glass, but delicate.

Sunflowers.

Amy Searle (13)
Stroud High School for Girls, Stroud

The Hunt

(Inspired by the painting 'The Hunt' by Monet)

Dogs straining on leads,
The hunters set out,
On a cold winter's morning,
No one about.

The sun's watery fingers,
Spread in the sky,
The group trailed footsteps behind them,
Snowflakes danced by.

On the frost-covered roofs,
Hung glass-like fingers of ice,
On top of the lake,
Sat a clear, frozen slice.

The hunters trudged past trees,
The branches grasping out,
To be saved from the howling,
Of the wind-wolf that's about.

Further into the forest,
The hunters' horses trot,
And through the snow-dusted branches,
The first innocent creature was shot.

Megan Evans (13)
Stroud High School for Girls, Stroud

Sunflowers

(Inspired by the painting 'Sunflowers' by Van Gogh)

Flaming sunflowers like faces
Never out of their perfect places
Golden, yellow, burning bright
Even in the dead of night.

Rusty centres as bright as the sun
But once their life is finished and done
The burning light will soon depart
They'll be sent off, empty of a heart.

But while their rusty centres glow
They will be praised from high and low
Petals as jagged as broken glass
As they expand among the grass.

Dejected, dead flowers
As the sunflowers tower
Delicate, spider-like petals
The stalks are made of metal.

Jagged petals like knotted hair
Make flowers that are oh so fair
Ragged, green leaves for this plant to be
The beauty of the sunflowers is plain to see.

Grace Walsh (13)
Stroud High School for Girls, Stroud

Sunflowers

(Inspired by the painting 'Sunflowers' by Van Gogh)

I see you
You see me
You are looking at me with your darkened faces
Haunting me
Throwing your yellow mane
Like you're laughing
You're standing still
Your legs can't move
But you're still swaying
Still watching
What are you waiting for?
I will out-stare you
You can't stop me
You pretend to turn away
Like you don't care
But I know you're still watching
Still waiting
Still haunting . . .

Alice Porter (13)
Stroud High School for Girls, Stroud

A Glowing Night

(Inspired by the painting 'Starry Night' by Van Gogh)

The stars like glowing beacons guided the waves,
A glowing night,
Rolling hills like waves,
Above a patchwork field of houses,
A sea of blue paint swallowing up the town,
Crashing, glowing, blue,
Curling, swirling, whirling,
The waves engulf the town.

Faye McCarthy (13)
Stroud High School for Girls, Stroud

When Klimt Painted The Kiss

(Inspired by the painting 'The Kiss' by Klimt)

When Klimt painted
What did he think of?
Was he dreaming an idle dream
Of a past happiness,
A fleeting moment,
Or wishing,
Or painting reality?
Were his colours real?
Gowns of red, black, gold and teal,
That hung like dream coats
Around the embrace,
Or were they a mere imagination,
A gathering of his life's
Colours and hues
Symbolising his hopes?
And was 'the kiss'
Real?

Gracie Dowling-Mardon (13)
Stroud High School for Girls, Stroud

Untitled

(Inspired By Monet's London)

The Parliament Houses, tall as man
Silhouetted against the calming sky
A light breeze, lighter than usual
Lazily shimmering the Thames
The sun burns a bonfire
As the buildings merge with air
The timid reflections of the violent sun
Join with the clouds' colour
Blood spills as silence fills
A dreadful act is done.

Ami Elliott
Stroud High School for Girls, Stroud

The Houses Of Parliament

(Inspired by Monet's Houses of Parliament)

How crowded,
Mixed-up and dull the place is,
How it is despised for hosting the country's conflicts,
If only it could be the possessor of debates instead of arguments,
Then it would be thought a lot more highly of for sure.

However,
At sunset,
It is transported to a whole new world,
A world full of sunlight, peace and tranquillity,
Where neither debates nor arguments take place,
Where people are bound to harmony.

Nevertheless,
No person could ever exist,
In a place so full of perfection,
They must live in reality.

And reality happens to involve the Houses of Parliament,
Where the sun never sets.

Rebecca Townsend (13)
Stroud High School for Girls, Stroud

Swan Girls

(Inspired by the painting 'Ballerina' by Degas)

A fan of feathers, radiating their swan-like beauty.
A dress of turquoise, green and yellow; fragile but graceful.
The elegant texture, the notion of walking on dreams.
Their copper-red hair; light shining off every facet.

The stage lights beam on, so powerful and bright.
Four ballerinas walk on and take their brittle poses.
Cutting through silence, one crisp note calls out; beckoning in all.
They start, moving in fluid movements, the audience captivated.

Ella Taylor-Seymour (13)
Stroud High School for Girls, Stroud

Time Is Dead

(Inspired by the painting 'Clocks' by Salvador Dali)

They lie melted across the floor
Covered in flies
The shine demolished
Nothing left but numbers
Time is completely forgot
Lost forever.

The tree stands motionless
No air is breathed
The buildings are grey with worry
As the cliffs crumble away
The world is silent
The time has come.

The sea ran away from the scene
Like a whimpering dog from a dead man
The rocks stood tall
And said nothing at all
The clocks are dead
The time has gone.

Lucie Chamberlain & Chloe Anderson-Dixon (13)
Stroud High School for Girls, Stroud

The Love Of Marriage

(Inspired by the painting 'The Married Couple' by Vermeer)

Newlyweds, both bride and groom,
Including a baby in her womb,
The evergreen tree,
The everlasting love,
As they float like doves,
To the egg-like sun,
The Eiffel Tower is a sapphire of blue,
Stretching beyond their reach.

Robyn Fletcher
Stroud High School for Girls, Stroud

Time

(Inspired by the painting 'Clocks' by Salvador Dali)

Time ticks by like there's no tomorrow,
Running on by without any sorrow,
Hanging on a branch,
Drying in the sun,
Melting, stretching, time.

Deep blue sea rushing on the beaches,
Secluded from the reaches of man,
Cliffs in the background,
Making not a sound,
Place full of sorrow.

Time stops ticking - there's no tomorrow,
Stops running by and cries for a while,
Slipping off the branch,
Then falls in a heap,
Tomorrow never comes.

Rebecca Waldram (13)
Stroud High School for Girls, Stroud

Time Is Running Out

(Inspired by the painting 'Clocks' by Salvador Dali)

The clocks drip sorrowfully,
They dangle sadly,
The sea and beach deserted,
Cliffs run smoothly,
Peaceful sand,
As lifeless as a grave,
The clocks hang, drip, slide,
And slip slowly,
The distorted face gives the eerie feel,
That time is running out.

Laura Paul (12)
Stroud High School for Girls, Stroud

Starry Night

(Inspired by the painting 'Starry Night' by Van Gogh)

The starry night starts at dusk,
As the sun begins to fade,
The town are all asleep,
When the stars appear in the evening shade.

The story of the midnight sky,
As the whirling clouds roll in,
All the trees become silhouettes,
With a dark, black atmosphere of sin.

The tiny town sits in twilight,
So helpless in this beauty,
The moon and stars look down on it,
Taking over with mutiny.

Instead of a clear sparkle,
The stars and moon will glow,
The mists will merge their light,
But still it's very clear, in the starry night.

Katie Lobley (13)
Stroud High School for Girls, Stroud

Black And White

Black and white.
A chequers board of life.
No mediator; just solid
Black and white.
Black road of darkness
White road of light
Black city of hatred
White city of purity
Black groom
White bride

And just one grey line dividing them.

Esther Harding (13)
Stroud High School for Girls, Stroud

Behind You

(Inspired by Rembrandt's self portrait)

Slow down to think
You'll be surprised what you find
Inside you you'll be surprised what you see.

I see you but you'll never see quite into me
I'm the island
The lull in the heart of the storm
Calm in the river of life.

I'm behind you all of the way
Though if you look, you won't ever see.

Slow down to think
To look and to find
But whenever you do
I'm standing behind.

If you ever break down
Lose it, feel like you're falling
I'm there
I'll catch you
Pick you up
Won't let you down
I'm the back-up plan you won't ever read
But I always fall into place.

Inside you
You'll be surprised to find me.

Lizzi Dunthorne (13)
Stroud High School for Girls, Stroud

Starry Night

(Inspired by the painting 'Starry Night' by Van Gogh)

With the moon that rose
Came a swirling mist
Through the cities' roads
It rolled in a twist

Although the mist was thick
The moonshine flooded the streets
Like a clever magic trick
As the stars rose up in fleets

The felled tree groaned
As the mist and wind rushed by
What little was left, it moaned
Gazing upon the city, it began to cry

Golds and blues and mist flashed high
The rolling hills rippled with light
Lit, shone up by the starry sky
Its thoughts were lost in the dance of the night.

Eleanor Linsell (13)
Stroud High School for Girls, Stroud

Picnic At The Riverside

Girls sit plaiting grass in the shade of the willow trees,
The sun burns down on women as they desperately attempt
To cover their bloodless faces, in fear of getting a tan.
All around, the young and old, rich and poor,
Relax on the velvet grass of the riverbank.
Occasionally, boats glide by,
Like feathers on the crystal river.
Dogs laze in the cooling shade,
As everyone feels the effects of the midday sun.

Hannah Staniforth (13)
Stroud High School for Girls, Stroud

Monet's London

(Inspired by Monet's London)

The sunset along the River Thames,
Was a most beautiful sight to see,
The river lapping against the wall of the church,
The sound like the inside of a shell.
It's like a sheet of silk, flowing, rippling,
And reflecting the buildings on the river's edge.
The colours of the river are as colourful as a rainbow,
With the mist spreading like a contagious disease,
With the dappled sun shining through.
The sunlight is like an explosion of fireworks,
Almost as if the sky is on fire.
The church's points are like daggers.
This is a building of spectacular architecture,
With the silhouette of it shining on the river.
The sun is shining through now,
Like a ball of fire glowing in the sky.

Lena Hey (13)
Stroud High School for Girls, Stroud

The Kiss

(Inspired by the painting 'The Kiss' by Klimt)

The woman is like a flower bed,
Her duvet is full of circles and curls,
She has a head of stars and flowers,
The swirls are smooth, bright and warm.

It's like a river of love,
Where clothes are like cloths of gold.

The man is like a block of concrete,
Colourful rectangles and squares,
The colours are oriental and bright,
He's solid and strong.

The picture is like a ball of love,
Where the man and woman are intertwined.

Hetta Leonard (13)
Stroud High School for Girls, Stroud

Sunlit Room

(Inspired by the painting 'The Married Couple' by Vermeer)

Hidden, by plumes of soft, emerald fabric
The start of a new generation
Haloed by the soft morning sunlight

The scarab of the church
Standing close by
Cast in shadow, is his form
Hiding what he truly is

Drapes of blood
All sinister and menacing
Concealing the truth about this meeting

A murderous plan?
A condemned couple?
Is this the last meeting of lovers?

A secret meeting in a room
Between a beauty and a beast
To be contained in this sunlit room.

Becky Megson (13)
Stroud High School for Girls, Stroud

As I Watch

(Inspired by the painting 'People By The Lake' by Seurat))

As I watch, the world slows down,
Trickling water slowly freezes.

For the first time, I see inside the citizens,
That rule and shape our lives.

I catch a glimpse of who they truly are,
That there is no difference between them,
That in living their lives as a mortal,
They are part of something bigger,
Something more than a mere creature on this Earth,
They are a piece in the puzzle of life.

Jess Cain (13)
Stroud High School for Girls, Stroud

Punting In The Sunset

(Inspired by Monet's London)

The brush stroked
Sweeping sunset sky,
Swooping low to the mysterious shadowy towers.

The burning sun,
Like a lighthouse,
Flickering into the shadows of night.

Fiery sun stretched thinly across the water,
With a boat soundlessly swimming,
Its fin sharply pointed,
Warningly,
Out of the sea.

A romantic time
For gliding peacefully
Along the still surface of the deep sea.

Laura Moreland
Stroud High School for Girls, Stroud

The Kiss

(Inspired by the painting 'The Kiss' by Klimt)

Passionate partners in a bed of gold,
Beautiful woman like a flower bed,
Sturdy, protecting man like a stone path,
Man and woman twisted together.

Curls and swirls encase their love,
Bright, oriental petals carry their love,
Stars in her hair symbolise her inner angel,
Gold clothing symbolises royalty.

The sunset setting prepares for romance,
As the sturdy man protects the precious woman,
They begin to kiss passionately,
And the everlasting river of love flows on.

Alice Fletcher (13)
Stroud High School for Girls, Stroud

Icarus

His wax wings slowly melted
From the great heat of the sun.
If he'd listened to his father's words
Flying might have been fun.

The sheep stood on the hillside
They knew not of his pain.
But at least there was something to ease his mind
He would not die in the rain.

He observed the land below
A man worked with his plough.
A teardrop fell from his open eye
He would never do that now.

His father watched from the sky above
He began to cry at his loss.
All the things his son would never do
The very thought made him cross.

As he hit the water
He saw fishes everywhere.
He saw great, green plants on the seabed
They got tangled in his hair.

His body hit the sea floor
In his lungs there was no air.
The life that once filled him, slowly left
And soon it wasn't there.

Martha Cunneen (13)
Stroud High School for Girls, Stroud

Time Is Hanging Out To Dry

(Inspired by the painting 'Clocks' by Salvador Dali)

The peaceful beach, quiet and deserted,
But for the face that lies undisturbed.

A washing line, time is hanging out to dry,
It's as lifeless as a graveyard,
But the cliff is still on guard,
Towering above, in the distance,
Watching over the plain of smooth mud.

With the box, all alone,
The sea has swept in company,
A lost sailor's possessions,
Whose time is running out.

Each drip is a tick,
Not long left,
For the sailor whose time,
Is hanging out to dry.

Laura Payling (12)
Stroud High School for Girls, Stroud

Winter In Austria

River stopped in mid-flow,
The houses covered in freak snow,
Boats stuck in mid-row.

Snow dancing to the ground,
Wrapping me in cold embrace,
Whispering close to my face,
I knew nothing of the secret,
Secret of the winter.

Bridges wrapped in their winter coats,
Black hands reach from the earth,
Grabbing at the snow,
Clutching it tight.

Sarah Nicol (13)
Stroud High School for Girls, Stroud

The Destruction

(Inspired by the painting 'Clocks' by Salvador Dali)

On a false look, an odd scene,
Quite calm and serene,
But hidden depths lie,
The fabric of time cannot deny.

The animal is a shattered dream,
Where time was soft, and ripped at the seam.
The fearful sun beats down,
Upon the convicted animal's frown.

The ocean lying in the background,
Is a warrior in ties, bound.
Fighting the desolate land,
The gloomy shadows lend no hand.

The clocks which melt,
Have undoubtedly felt,
The burn of the flaming sun,
Whose pain cannot be undone.

The hand of the clock is a brittle pin,
Sadly defeated, there is no win.
The animal lying limp, lost,
He leaves nature but at what cost?

Time, technology, they all had their part,
But the jagged daggers of the mountain are smart.
The Earth shall win,
Before the destruction will begin.

Jessica Gibson (13)
Stroud High School for Girls, Stroud

The Place Of Time

(Inspired by the painting 'Clocks' by Salvador Dali)

The tiny, timeless clock hands pass by minutes as road signs on a
dirt track.

While it's melting, friends silently slip away.
The dripping watch hangs over a spiny branch as a saddle sits on
a racehorse.

Mirages whisper and scuttle past,
Dark is nearing, coming fast.
The lifeless swan lies still in a stretched-out sheet,
As an old tattered blanket is draped on a child's bed.
While angels taint its tortured soul,
It dissolves so softly into the empty, brown carpet.
For death itself, like quicksand waits,
'Neath the glassed table it lies,
Invisible to human eyes.
The pristine, petite locket stopwatch falls like a gold coin in the sand,
Posed, open, sneaks upon your sight.
Not remembered are the fragile leaves,
Nor the grassy plains destructible.
Desert sands sip distant waters,
Split mountains creep beyond the horizon.
To worlds where old dreams come anew,
The solemn atmosphere continues,
While time itself forgotten too.

Amber Cornock
Stroud High School for Girls, Stroud

Think

Can you see the cold sea rippling and the last, tired fishermen
catching their fish?
Can you see the reflection of the dark blue sky?
But which is which, sky or sea?
Can you see the red-hot sun fall like a golden shooting star in the
midnight darkness?
Is the slow, sleepy sun ever going to stop and think about its day,
or even stop falling?
What do you think? The water, the boats, the sky, the setting sun,
what do you see?
Maybe sorrow, love or even happiness, it's your choice.
The sea is blue, the sun is red, the fishing boats are gliding like
a swan.
Still, can you feel the breeze whipping through your hair?
Can it be gentle or firm? Let me think, or better yet, tell me what
you think.
Just remember to think!

Jenna Day (12)
Stroud High School for Girls, Stroud

H I M

A dark shadow, creeping through the trees
The sound of pain through a child's cry, his speech
The dark room full of pain, his lair
The touch of his hand, as frozen as ice
The hardness of his heart, which cannot fill with love
The sharp stare from his eyes never ends
The colour of his skin so pale, as if dead
The life he leads, the evil
Now he sleeps, so silent.

Bryony Thomas & Jo Tolley
Stroud High School for Girls, Stroud

Golden Sunflowers

(Inspired by the painting 'Sunflowers' by Van Gogh)

Sunflowers, orange, yellow, and as bright as the sun,
Their heads as round as milk bottle lids,
The stems give the impression the flowers are as tall as giants.

They are in a room, positioned on a golden table,
Sparkling in the sun like crystals.
The room around them is as blue as the sky.

The flowers in the vase, upright like models on a stage,
As still as statues,
Some standing, others bending as if carrying heavy weights.

The vase they are situated in, is as yellow as lemons,
Flowers lean over the edge like spectators at a football match,
Leaves also peer over the edge as green as limes,
They dance and prance in the sudden gust of wind,
And then return to their set positions,
Giving the impression they are dead.

Charlotte Brookfield (12)
Stroud High School for Girls, Stroud

Forgotten

I cannot imagine a life other than this,
To interact with people, to talk and to kiss.

But instead I sit here, watching life go by,
Whilst I sit in this room, all I do is cry.

Stuck in this room all day and all night,
I've forgotten how to act, what's wrong and what's right.

Time carries on, yet I stay the same,
I'm completely forgotten, no one knows my name.

The walls are closing in, I'm running out of air,
If only someone noticed me, if only someone cared.

Amy Dipple (13)
Stroud High School for Girls, Stroud

The Tower Through The Mist

There's the tower through the mist,
Subtle, still and secretive.
No one knows the truth,
About the tower through the mist.

There's the setting sun,
You can see it on the sea.
No one knows the magic,
Well nobody but me.

Through the years it's been there,
Through the years has it.
Now blurred by the mist,
Less visible bit by bit.

There was magic in that tower,
Happiness and joy.
The old man and his wife,
Me, the little boy.

We lived in that tower,
We loved that tower.
In it we stayed,
Through the darkest hour.

They came in, they killed them,
They wanted it all.
But they lost their lives,
At the tower's creepy call.

There was magic in that tower,
Pure and sweet back then.
But all is lost now,
Through the sin of men.
The tower through the mist.

Eleanor Pontac (13)
Stroud High School for Girls, Stroud

Lost Love

For the love that's lost
I sit and wait
For days and nights
I sit and wait
One more drink
I sit and wait
After this last one
He'll be at the door
I sit and wait.

For every drunk that comes in here
I sit and wait
For every cop that threatens
I sit and wait
For every trigger pulled
I sit and wait
Just hoping he's gonna come
Back through that door
Like he promised he would
I sit and wait.

Deep down I know he won't
The last time I saw him
Drunk, tired, emotional
Chain-smoking
Stripped off his shirt
Stuck flowers down his trousers
Danced down the lamp-lit road
Gone forever.

Rachael Merrett (13)
Stroud High School for Girls, Stroud

The Roar

It rains long and hard,
All is still, nothing moves,
But the brambles and the gorse
Waving in the breeze.

It rains long and hard,
Plink-plonk on the metal,
The iron rumbles,
The bridge begins to shake.

The track is humming,
Hear it coming,
A roar of metal, steam and smoke,
A hot metal monster,
Eating up the track,
Faster, faster,
Hinges creaking,
Metal's under pressure,
Cor! They reek,
Crashing water underneath,
A moment screaming with power and pain,
And yet . . .
Only a moment.

It rains long and hard,
Plink-plonk on the cooling metal,
There is no movement,
But the brambles and gorse
Waving in the breeze.

Grace Cooper (13)
Stroud High School for Girls, Stroud

Time, Goodbye

(Inspired by the painting 'Clocks' by Salvador Dali)

Time is slipping
Time is dripping
Draped over a branch
Hung out to dry

Time is seeing
Time is fleeing
They, as people, stand as spectators
Watching time pass us by

Time is falling
Time is calling
No one but I
Realises the dreaded fate
We have no time

Time is going
Time has gone
As quiet as the night
They wait to hear its return
But no sound is heard
As they realise their time has come
And their time has gone.

Natasha Longwill (13)
Stroud High School for Girls, Stroud

The Window

I look through my frosted window,
I try to paint the ice skaters' moods,
But the darkness of the sky
Dampens their joy,
And instead brings sadness and melancholy.
Past the snow-capped mountains,
On top of an icy hill,
Stand five hunters.
I see a bird hover in the mist,
It is dark, like a shadow on the ground.
The hunters raise their guns,
The bird drops silently,
To the floor.
I only just capture it in the sky,
But knowing it is gone.
I look at my pathetic canvas,
All I see is gloom.
This picture is my life.
I sit here,
Watching through my window,
Mesmerised, lonely.

Bethan Beckett (13)
Stroud High School for Girls, Stroud

Marriage And Divorce

M an and wife
A ctions speak louder than words
R elated families
R ange of people at the service
I mportant day
A ffection for one another
G reat outfits
E verlasting love

D eparture from marriage
I nsensitive behaviour
V ariety of hatred
O utrageous money
R efusal to commit
C ourt case
E nd of love.

Vicky Bourne & Abbie Parker (13)
Stroud High School for Girls, Stroud

Island

Soft sand beneath me
Followed by the deep blue sea
The ships are full sail
Thrashing through the sparkling water
The waves lap up to the beach.

The sun beating down
The cool sea breeze
Blowing through my hair cools me off
The waves come splashing
Then I smoothly jump into the chilled blue sea.

So refreshing, yet so calm
The place to relax.

The tranquillity runs through me
Never stopping . . .

Emma Hart (13)
Stroud High School for Girls, Stroud

Trouble

Don't make trouble
Don't make agitation
Don't annoy the neighbours
And don't cause irritation . . .

This is what my mum says
Before she goes out
But when she returns
She knows without a doubt . . .

I have made bother
I have made discord
I did all this because
I was really bored.

This causes misfortune
This causes sorrow
This suffering is over now
Until tomorrow!

Laura Atkins (13)
Stroud High School for Girls, Stroud

Birthday

B rilliant day
I ndividual day
R epeated day
T errific day
H appy day
D elightful day
A we-inspiring day
Y outhful day.

Kelly Jones (13)
Stroud High School for Girls, Stroud

The Pharaoh Sleeps

The Egyptian pharaoh lies in peace,
Life is frozen but not dead,
The slender mantis creeps,
Graceful and slow,
Its legs so pin-like,
Tiptoe across the body of its victim.

It is dark, very dark,
Lit only by the shimmering stars ahead,
But the mantis pierces this dead of night,
Like a fatal knife to skin.

The pharaoh lies in his bed,
An archway curves across, framing the sky,
The grand columns are rippled,
Like the sea's gentle waves,
Silence fills the emptiness,
But life is frozen, not dead . . .

Rachel Bell (13)
Stroud High School for Girls, Stroud

Empty

An empty bar
An empty street
An empty glass
An empty seat.

An empty heart
An empty soul
Any empty life
Like a black hole.

Alex Flett (13)
Stroud High School for Girls, Stroud

The Journey

Crawling down the valley, scrambling across the track,
Chugging through the fog, no way back.

Water rippling calmly, boats bobbing smoothly,
Chugging through the fog, stumbling up the track.

Coughing through the dust, grabbing at the rails,
Like crawling up a ladder, clambering along the track.

Puffing smoke and whistling, like a kettle boiling,
Feeble lights are guiding, lost amongst the tracks.

Emerging from the mist, passing through the fog,
Reaching final destination, leaving the forbidding track.

Now there is no way back.

No way back.

Back.

Robyn Brown (13)
Stroud High School for Girls, Stroud

The Dancers

My feet are aching, my heart is beating,
My pale skin sweating, my thin bones trembling,
Locks of fire around my head,
A flush of blue on my tutu.
We're all in a line, not ready to go,
We take a deep breath to dance in the show.

Amber Flexen-Cook (13)
Stroud High School for Girls, Stroud

Tearaway Teen

What is beneath the surface cannot be seen,
These are the feelings of a tearaway teen.
The calm blue oceans are deeper than you and I can see,
It hides its truths and sorrows from you and me.

Why do people play with our emotions, are we not humans too?
Or are we asinine toys to pick up and throw out depending on
one's mood?
Why was I treated differently from her, him or you?
Was I abnormal, a freak show, or were you just confused?

I may be cynical and have a defiant attitude,
Try to elucidate what convinced you to make this astute move.
I want to understand, it turned me into who I am today,
Someone who lost their confidence, but someone with a lot to say.

I'm two years older now, what do you expect?
What was it you always said? Keep the family's respect?
That's all you cared about - not me, just you,
That's why you're lonely and by the sound of it, still selfish too.

Reminiscing about all the memories and the past I've left behind,
It seems as though I watch life aimlessly passing me by.
The world still spinning, the clock still ticking and I'm a victim of
this time,
But don't you agonise about this era, it's not for you to seize,
it's mine.

At times I just wanted somewhere to run and hide, if only for a while.
Why are we all incompetent victims of God's cunning trial?
I thought things would improve. No! It will always stay the same,
I no longer require your concern as I have learnt how to play life's
harsh game.

Neetz Grewal
Swakeleys School, Uxbridge

The Playground

I walked out of my classroom, some money in my hand,
I sat down on a bench, near a pit of sand.
I took out some paper and started to draw,
And when I looked up, I stared in awe.
'Give me the money,' the boy started to shout,
I called for a teacher, no one about.
I looked at the money, stone-cold in my hand,
And put away my paper that lay softly on the sand.
'No,' I said firmly, my fist screwed up tight,
And I raised it up and threatened a fight.
The boy started to laugh, then his fist raised up too,
But got no further than an inch or so.
'Stop right there,' the teacher shouted out,
'You two are up to mischief, I know that without a doubt.'
She looked at the money and then at the boy,
She looked at my face, it was sad, without joy.
She sent him to the headmaster, his head hanging low,
And looked at me graciously, said 'There's something you
should know.'
I looked at her puzzled, what did she mean?
She said, *'Never be afraid of bullies, because it makes them keen!'*

Beatrice Baranowska (12)
Swanmead Community School, Ilminster

The Deserted House And The Wood

There once was a house on the edge of a wood,
A deserted thatched house on the edge of the wood,
And the reason the house was the way that it was,
Was because of a murder in the house in the wood.
An old man had murdered his wife, it is said,
In that old, run-down house, in his poor wife's own bed.
He stabbed her to death and the whole world turned red,
And her ghost jumped out of her on her old bed.
It wanders the house and also the wood,
And now no one goes there, or that spooky old wood.

Lucy Dillon (12)
Swanmead Community School, Ilminster

No Nonsense

In the sea
In the town
I don't really care
As long as I am with my friends
And I can wash my hair.

At my house
In the sky
I don't really care
As long as I have a book to read
And I am curled up on my chair.

In a tree
Underground
I don't really care
As long as I have a strawberry to eat
And lots and lots of cream.

On the sand
In my class
I don't really care
As long as I have a TV to watch
And the sun is beaming on my hair.

Ellen Morris Storey (12)
Swanmead Community School, Ilminster

The Selfish World

In the world in which we live,
Why do we take and not give?
Why do millions of children die?
Because of hunger, AIDS and selfish lives.

Why do children work hard all day,
When we go to school and play?
Why don't other countries help Africa?
Instead of letting it wither and die.

Abigail Smith (12)
Swanmead Community School, Ilminster

What Would It Be Like To Be A Rabbit?

Would you like to be a rabbit?
Small, grey, with your whole life in front of you?
Just wait and see.
There would be so much danger around you.
Stop! There's something behind you.
It's a fox! Run for it rabbit,
Run for it, run for it, run, run, run.
Quick, back to your house.
You're nearly there when there's a shadow above . . .
Oh no! it's a buzzard!
Suddenly your whole life flashes before you,
With your last steps to safety.

Katy Brown (12)
Swanmead Community School, Ilminster

Poverty

The rest of the world is suffering with poverty
We need to make sure it's history
Can we ensure longevity?
The life and feelings of others is a mystery
Everyone needs help all over the Earth
We are beginning to realise the suffering
Are attempting to encourage mirth
Everyone should always be giving
They are there suffering with starvation
They are always searching for hope
We will always be making communications
We will help and they will cope
This isn't fake, this is their story
Poverty can and will be history!

Lorna Rainey (13)
The Cotswold School, Bourton-on-the-Water

A Vision Of Arya

Green eyes
Black hair
Staring at me
That deep green stare.

Pale skin
Slim form
Moonbeams trapped in her midnight hair
Waiting for the first light of dawn.

Lean face
Angled brows
Elfin fair
Like white as winter snows.

She stares right at me
Chills go up my spine
The hairs stand up on the back of my neck
Like needle jabs along a dotted line.

It strikes me the way
She holds her head high
But it won't hide the fact
That she's going to cry.

She turns back away from me
To let fall her tears
I know that her death
Would be the sum of my fears.

James Ager (13)
The Cotswold School, Bourton-on-the-Water

My Meggie

I love my little puppy,
Her coat's so soft and warm,
She bounces round the garden,
Then flops down on the lawn.
Because she's still a baby,
She sleeps for most of the day,
But when it comes to bedtime,
She wants to awake and play.
Meggie is learning quite quickly,
To go outside and tiddle,
But she needs to learn quicker,
I'm not the one to nibble.
We've waited such a long time,
To get our bundle of fluff,
But it was really worth the wait,
And life is not so tough.

Laura Osgood (12)
The Cotswold School, Bourton-on-the-Water

Stress

I'm sitting on cloud nine,
Thinking about my day,
I wish it could be fine,
And wipe it all away.

My hair is all in scraggs,
Caused by all the stress,
I feel like a pile of rags,
I feel like tearing my dress.

I wish my problem was water,
I'd pour it down the drain,
The problems feel like slaughter,
It's driving me insane!

I've thought about my day
And have wiped it all away.

Laura McNamara (13)
The Cotswold School, Bourton-on-the-Water

If I Had A Dream

In my dream . . .

I would make world peace between countries,
Also families and friends.
I would make everyone recycle
And know what's happening to the world and care for it.
I would make poverty history
And let everyone and everything be fair.
I would keep the memory and soul alive forever,
The one of my grampy and others' loved ones.
I would make everyone happy, caring, kind and thoughtful
And think of other people.
I would put bullies and people that hurt others
In a place where no one could get hurt.
I would make everyone feel happy about themselves
And have everlasting confidence.
I would make everyone appreciate what they have got
And look after people that they love.
I would make people who are great people die when they need to
And with love in their heart.
I would think people would agree with me on what I dream about,
But if you have a dream, then do it and live life to the full!

Katie Fifield (12)
The Cotswold School, Bourton-on-the-Water

Why?

People killing, dying, starving, why?
Hate overrules love, why?
Drugs, violence, murder, why?
Greed, anger, jealousy, why?
Poverty, war, terrorists, why?
Why is the world falling apart?
Why?

Hannah Apperley (12)
The Cotswold School, Bourton-on-the-Water

Poem Of A Poem

Pieces of beauty flowing down the page,
Pile loads of symbolism in its own way.
Each word significant to the writer's thought,
Each sentence needed a minute's worth pause.

All the illustrations running through your mind,
Lots of colours swirling in your eyes,
There are lots of thoughts to find.
Guess what it is, a poem of my mind.

Emma Nevins (13)
The Cotswold School, Bourton-on-the-Water

The Haunted Room

Cobwebs hanging as water falls,
Old paperwork, dusty walls,
Flickering lights, shadows show,
Windows open, curtains blow.

This room looks scary,
Bad and old,
I think it's haunted
Well, that's what I was told.

Latoya Evans (13)
The Cotswold School, Bourton-on-the-Water

Poem

The moon shines on our pool
And this makes pictures on our wall
The branches sway lightly in the wind
And this makes us want to swim.

We splash around
As the moon goes down
We grab our clothes
And go downtown.

Jamie Dyer (13)
The Cotswold School, Bourton-on-the-Water

War

Bang! Silence. Bang! I look around and see death,
Death is there everywhere, staring at you,
Bodies are forgotten, led there and left,
All the bodies rotting, blood soaked right through,
Your mind is full of images, nothing else,
Poppies all around staining the floor like blood,
I bend down, on my hand there lay a louse,
Imprints of bodies moulded in mud,
War is all around us, causing hell,
Comparing this war is not really possible,
No one can stand the sight and stingy smell,
Fighting isn't fun and pleasure at all,
Bang! Bang! Bang! is all I hear. Bang! Bang! Bang!
'God save our King' is what the soldiers sang.

Holly Gardner (13)
The Cotswold School, Bourton-on-the-Water

The Refugee

Where's the peace in the world?
There's hurt wherever I look
When I saw it I nearly hurled
Coz it was in my mind it stuck
I only saw the refugees
Being killed right and left
They were on their knees
Being accused of all the theft
They tortured prisoners out of their minds
The public were waving white flags
But they tortured them till they were blind
Everyone was walking round in rags
I saw someone take their last breath
As they tumbled to their death.

Katherine Bentham (13)
The Cotswold School, Bourton-on-the-Water

Light Vs Dark

On the good side there is light
Whereas on the side of evil there is dark
All they want to do all day is fight
Whereas all the light think day is a lark
All they want is fun
And to muck around in the sun
Whereas in the night
The darkness think that really bites
It would drive me round the bend
If all the clashing were to end
I don't want any of it to change
Otherwise peace and hope would be out of our range.

Tom Cairns (13)
The Cotswold School, Bourton-on-the-Water

The Fox Hunt

The fox is like a bullet in the wind
When you shoot it sprints away
They're on their hunting horses
As they ride, ride away
Many agree, others think like me
The hounds are like guinea pigs
They're only there to chase the foxes.

Luke Tallon (12)
The Cotswold School, Bourton-on-the-Water

Waterfalls

Each tiny droplet falls gracefully over the rocks.
Autumnal colours surround the beautiful purity,
As it glides towards the earth.
I watch as the sun reflects off several beads,
Making them twinkle in the rays.
Such peace I find here, next to my waterfall.

Megan Stokes (14)
The King Alfred School, Highbridge

I Feel Like A . . .

(Inspired by 'I Feel Like a Suitcase' by John Hegley)

I feel like a table
I get scratched, cut
And people put gum on me
I get stood on
Most of the time people mistreat me
And break me and draw on me
I wish I hadn't ever been made.

Stephen Lewis (14)
The King Alfred School, Highbridge

Zoo - Haikus

Pacing forever,
Wide eyes gaze in wonderment,
Emptiness deepens.

Mounting depression,
Boredom and anxiety,
Pacing forever.

Bethany Aylward (14)
The King Alfred School, Highbridge

I Feel Like A Bottle . . .

(Inspired by 'I Feel Like a Suitcase' by John Hegley)

I feel like a bottle
People always bite me
I get really annoyed
They use me
Then abuse me
I'm so fed up
I could spill
And roll away.

Stephanie Smith (14)
The King Alfred School, Highbridge

I Feel Like A . . .

(Inspired by 'I Feel Like a Suitcase' by John Hegley)

I feel like a BMX racing bike
My wheels get tired and wear down
My rubber goes because I ride so much
My frame is dented and chipped
But I've just been given new brakes
I've travelled to Holland
And raced against many other BMXs
I hope Dan doesn't trade me in.

Dan Tipton (14)
The King Alfred School, Highbridge

I Feel Like A Car

(Inspired by 'I Feel Like a Suitcase' by John Hegley)

I feel like a car
Always running over tar
When it is hot
I melt like a chocolate bar

I feel like I am abused
When I am used
I have to run miles
While I'm carrying people.

Craig Tanner (14)
The King Alfred School, Highbridge

I Feel Like A . . .

(Inspired by 'I Feel Like a Suitcase' by John Hegley)

I feel like a car
I get revved too much all the time
I go the same way all the time
They always wait until I'm out of oil
And then wonder why I won't start
Because I'm used, abused and knackered.

William Puddy (14)
The King Alfred School, Highbridge

Waterfalls

Flowing by endlessly
Day after day
Gushing past constantly
Always without a delay

Swirling white water plummets
It froths and foams
Where it falls down in torrents
As it crashes and breaks to find a home

Bashing unmercifully on the rocks
It never stops
Much unlike the water in docks
Where people are on boats with mops

The water glistens as it reflects the sun
With sparkles and a shimmer
A cloud covers the sun though the water will still run
As it lands murkily like when the sun grows dimmer

It still rushes on in an endless flow
Never truly gone
Who knows where the mighty river will go
But still the water rushes on . . .

Emily Frost (14)
The King Alfred School, Highbridge

Waterfall

The leaf lands gently onto the flow,
Silently gliding along the stream.
It follows the unwritten map towards the meet,
All gathering as one.

The water cascades over a rock,
Smothering it in a cold blanket,
It bends sharply, the leaf slips under,
Never to be seen again.

Riordan Cooper (14)
The King Alfred School, Highbridge

The Zoo

The elephant lies upon the ground
As the keeper keeps him clean
He looks around his large compound
And doesn't care about looking mean.

The tiger on the other hand
Is walking, ready to prance
He walks up and down on the sand
He does not want to dance.

The monkeys swing to and fro
As the babies hold on tight
The youngest swings so very low
The others start to play fight.

The zoo changes every day
As the animals act in such different ways.

Claire Polly (14)
The King Alfred School, Highbridge

Waterfalls

The never-ending cycle,
Falling, crashing upon rocks,
Tumbling down crevices.

It is the natural beauty of the country,
Calm and soothing,
Anger is nowhere.

To cliffs it is destructive,
Wearing them away,
Destroying.

Christopher Coggins (14)
The King Alfred School, Highbridge

Waterfalls

Surrounded by hillsides, hid down in the valley,
Determined to find its way through,
The waterfall pushes through everything,
Not knowing what to do.

Spraying as it hits the rocks,
Drowning everything in its way,
The water gushes past again,
Getting larger every day.

As the sun begins to set,
The water starts to calm,
Silently resting in its place,
Just waiting for the alarm.

The sun has once again risen,
The journey is carried on,
The snake-like path of water,
On which the sun's reflection shone.

The surroundings bow down,
To the water in sight,
Every layer from layer,
To incredible heights.

The never-ending whirling water,
Moans as the lightning strikes,
Time to move on quicker now,
Not able to move as it likes.

Soon the journey will at long last end,
The waterfall can now rest,
For now it softly whispers,
To the animals in the west.

Kayleigh Gillard (14)
The King Alfred School, Highbridge

Waterfalls

Gushing fast, can you see?
It's wild and running free.
No one speaks, just looks upon,
For it's always there and never gone.

Nature's creation beautifully runs,
Up and down in its tons,
A layer of water never-ending,
Twisting, turning and bending.

Peaceful, relaxing, in one rush,
It's like a million people saying 'hush',
The sun shines on the flowing waterfall,
It shimmers as it crashes against its walls.

At places when it is slow,
You can see what's down below,
Radiant fishes swim so gracefully,
But the water moves them along as if a bully.

The wall of water is slowly surrounded by darkness
And a different beauty is presented.
The peacefulness is accompanied by night,
And the water moves in the moon's light.

Tara Moxey (14)
The King Alfred School, Highbridge

Waterfall - Haiku

So calm but angry
So full of strange emotions
Never-ending pain.

Oliver Cocking (13)
The King Alfred School, Highbridge

The Zoo - The Hell

Sluggish, lazy, non-existence,
Pacing to and fro, to and fro.
People stare and jeer at me,
They don't even know.

My home before was stunning,
I was free to run, hunt and play.
No people, crowds or staring,
Just me lazing all the day.

Cruelly, I was ripped from my land,
And placed here on display.
The Devil's captive,
Flaunted in Hell in such an awful way.

Lynsey Wilson (14)
The King Alfred School, Highbridge

The Waterfall - Haiku

It goes on and on
The ongoing waterfall
It goes on and on.

Dan Reynolds (14)
The King Alfred School, Highbridge

The Zoo - Haiku

Tourists gawp at me,
Trapped inside these metal bars,
I'm an 'attraction'.

Kerry Matthews (14)
The King Alfred School, Highbridge

Waterfalls

Wherever you are,
Always a sound,
Turning of water,
Escalating around.

Rampant waves,
Glistening light,
Through the day,
A beautiful sight.

Never-ending,
Nature's home,
And on the top,
Pearly foam.

And as you walk,
Through nature's path,
Admire the surroundings,
As you pass.

Leona Walsh (14)
The King Alfred School, Highbridge

Elevators

Off the train, crammed in pain,
Then another kerfuffle,
Kids screaming,
Mother shouting,
Businessmen talking,
Homeless begging,
Elevator whirring,
Queue forming,
Elevator whirring,
Surfacing from underneath,
Still, elevator whirling.

Robert Ireland (14)
The King Alfred School, Highbridge

The Zoo

Monkeys swinging in the trees,
Doing whatever they please,
Eating bananas and lounging about,
Until the zookeepers do shout.

Tigers prowl around their cages,
They've been stuck in here for ages,
Boredom sets in twenty-four seven,
They can't wait till they go to tiger heaven.

Elephants stomp up and down,
On their faces a constant frown,
Toes being filed down every day,
Oh, why does it have to be this way?

Eventually the light fades away,
And so begins another day.

Christopher Brown (14)
The King Alfred School, Highbridge

The Zoo

In the zoo the tigers pace
Boredom's written all over their face

The monkeys fight in agitation
They'd sooner be in their home nation

An elephant lies down on the floor
His toenails shorter than before

Lions lying all day long
Keeping animals like this is wrong.

Lewis Hassall (14)
The King Alfred School, Highbridge

The Waterfall

Water, water all around,
Water, water, the only sound,
Crashing on the rocks below,
In the wind, the rain or the snow,
This relaxing motion will always flow.

It flows so freely,
So sweetly,
So softly,
Until it gets to the sheer drop,
Straight across,
Then over the top.

Over it goes,
Crashing to the ground,
If no one's around,
Does it make a sound?

Danielle Hughes (14)
The King Alfred School, Highbridge